What Impact Does Mental Illness Have on Violent Crime?

Patricia D. Netzley

INCONTROVERSY

ReferencePoint
Press®

San Diego, CA

© 2015 ReferencePoint Press, Inc.
Printed in the United States

For more information, contact:
ReferencePoint Press, Inc.
PO Box 27779
San Diego, CA 92198
www. ReferencePointPress.com

LIBRARY OF CONGRESS CATALOGING-IN-PUBLICATION DATA

Netzley, Patricia D.
    What impact does mental illness have on violent crime? / by Patricia D. Netzley.
        pages cm. — (In controversy)
    Audience: Grade 9 to 12
    Includes bibliographical references and index.
    ISBN 978-1-60152-660-1 (hardback) — ISBN 1-60152-660-1 (hardback)
    1. Mentally ill offenders—United States—Juvenile literature. 2. Criminals—Mental health—United States—Juvenile literature. I. Title.
    HV6133.N48   2014
    364.2'4--dc23
                                                                                    2013046949

Contents

Foreword

I n 2008, as the US economy and economies worldwide were falling into the worst recession since the Great Depression, most Americans had difficulty comprehending the complexity, magnitude, and scope of what was happening. As is often the case with a complex, controversial issue such as this historic global economic recession, looking at the problem as a whole can be overwhelming and often does not lead to understanding. One way to better comprehend such a large issue or event is to break it into smaller parts. The intricacies of global economic recession may be difficult to understand, but one can gain insight by instead beginning with an individual contributing factor, such as the real estate market. When examined through a narrower lens, complex issues become clearer and easier to evaluate.

This is the idea behind ReferencePoint Press's *In Controversy* series. The series examines the complex, controversial issues of the day by breaking them into smaller pieces. Rather than looking at the stem cell research debate as a whole, a title would examine an important aspect of the debate such as *Is Stem Cell Research Necessary?* or *Is Embryonic Stem Cell Research Ethical?* By studying the central issues of the debate individually, researchers gain a more solid and focused understanding of the topic as a whole.

Each book in the series provides a clear, insightful discussion of the issues, integrating facts and a variety of contrasting opinions for a solid, balanced perspective. Personal accounts and direct quotes from academic and professional experts, advocacy groups, politicians, and others enhance the narrative. Sidebars add depth to the discussion by expanding on important ideas and events. For quick reference, a list of key facts concludes every chapter. Source notes, an annotated organizations list, bibliography, and index provide student researchers with additional tools for papers and class discussion.

The *In Controversy* series also challenges students to think critically about issues, to improve their problem-solving skills, and to sharpen their ability to form educated opinions. As President Barack Obama stated in a March 2009 speech, success in the twenty-first century will not be measurable merely by students' ability to "fill in a bubble on a test but whether they possess 21st century skills like problem-solving and critical thinking and entrepreneurship and creativity." Those who possess these skills will have a strong foundation for whatever lies ahead.

No one can know for certain what sort of world awaits today's students. What we can assume, however, is that those who are inquisitive about a wide range of issues; open-minded to divergent views; aware of bias and opinion; and able to reason, reflect, and reconsider will be best prepared for the future. As the international development organization Oxfam notes, "Today's young people will grow up to be the citizens of the future: but what that future holds for them is uncertain. We can be quite confident, however, that they will be faced with decisions about a wide range of issues on which people have differing, contradictory views. If they are to develop as global citizens all young people should have the opportunity to engage with these controversial issues."

In Controversy helps today's students better prepare for tomorrow. An understanding of the complex issues that drive our world and the ability to think critically about them are essential components of contributing, competing, and succeeding in the twenty-first century.

Contributing to Violence?

On September 16, 2013, former navy petty officer Aaron Alexis went to the headquarters of the Naval Sea Systems Command within the Washington Navy Yard in Washington, DC, armed with a 12-gauge shotgun. Two days earlier he had purchased the gun and two boxes of shells after being subjected to a state and federal background check that showed that he had never been convicted of a crime or declared mentally ill in a court of law. However, he was not allowed to carry the gun into the naval yard, so he hid it, disassembled, inside a backpack. He then went to Building 197, a secure facility where he had previously been working as a civilian contractor, and reassembled the gun in a bathroom before starting to shoot people throughout the building.

Alexis fired seemingly at random, hitting most of his victims in the head, and after killing a security guard he took the man's semi-automatic handgun and continued his assault with that weapon. Nearly an hour after Alexis first entered the building, he engaged in a firefight with police that lasted more than thirty minutes. A man who was hiding with coworkers in a nearby office subsequently described it, saying, "It was a fierce, major gun battle. Bullets were flying through my office, over our heads, and kept going for minutes. Then I heard, 'Shooter down. Shooter down.'"[1] Alexis was dead. Ultimately twelve of his victims also died; eight others were injured.

Low-Frequency Electromagnetic Waves

After the Navy Yard shooting, people struggled to come up with reasons for Alexis to have committed this violent act, especially since he was a practicing Buddhist known for promoting peace.

Some said that he had been involved in a monetary dispute with the company employing him and was in serious debt, suggesting that stress and anger over his situation might have caused him to snap. Indeed, his father reported that Alexis sometimes had bursts of anger because he suffered from a stress disorder caused by rescuing victims of the 9/11 terrorist attacks in New York in 2001.

This anger was evident in two incidents that came to the attention of police. In 2004 Alexis shot out the tires of a truck while in a rage over a parking dispute and later claimed he could not remember doing it. In 2010 he fired a gun into the ceiling of his apartment, sending a bullet into the apartment of an upstairs neighbor with whom he had quarreled over how noisy she was, but he insisted that he had fired accidentally while cleaning his gun.

However, as the investigation into the mass shooting progressed, officials discovered that Alexis had more than just anger problems. On August 7, 2013, he had called police to his hotel room in Newport, Rhode Island, to report that three people were transmitting voices into his head using low-frequency electromagnetic waves. He insisted that he had heard these voices coming through the floor, walls, and/or ceiling while in two other hotels as well, including one on a naval base, and that the culprits were using a microwave to bombard him with vibrations that kept him awake.

Later that month Alexis sought treatment twice at a Veterans Administration hospital emergency room for his insomnia, but because he did not seem mentally ill, he was simply given medication to help him sleep and told to follow up with a primary care physician, which he never did. Unfortunately this scenario is not uncommon. According to analyses in 2013 by the *New York Times* and *Mother Jones* magazine, although the majority of people responsible for shooting rampages are mentally ill, most had not yet been diagnosed as mentally ill at the time of the shooting.

A Growing Problem

The National Alliance on Mental Illness defines mental illnesses as "conditions that disrupt a person's thinking, feeling, mood, ability to relate to others and daily functioning."[2] There are many types of mental illnesses, only a few of them associated with the level of

An FBI photograph shows Aaron Alexis, shotgun in hand, stalking the hallway of Building 197 at the Washington (DC) Navy Yard in September 2013. Alexis killed twelve people and injured eight others before being shot dead.

violence that Alexis exhibited. But although the majority of ill-nesses show no apparent connection to violence, statistics suggest that mass shootings by mentally ill individuals are on the rise. According to *Mother Jones* magazine, before 1999 there were roughly one hundred such shootings, but seventy-three of these took place after 1990, and an additional thirty-three such cases took place after 2000, up to and including the Navy Yard shooting.

People disagree on why more mass shootings take place in America today than in years past. Some say it is because the modern media glorify violence and reward criminal behavior with fame. Others say it is because there are not enough gun control laws to prevent violent and/or mentally ill individuals from gaining access to weapons. Still others say that even if these things are true, the main fault lies with America's mental health system. In fact, a Gallup poll reported in September 2013 that 80 percent of Americans blamed mass shootings on a failure of the mental health system to identify individuals who are a danger to others.

Some people suggest that the problem is not just one of identification but also of treatment. Mona Charen, a columnist with the *Chicago Sun-Times*, states:

> We have betrayed the mentally ill by drastically reducing the availability of treatment. America has roughly 5 percent of the psychiatric beds it had in the late 1950s. When Aaron Alexis called police in Rhode Island last month and complained of "voices" in his head and the "people who were sending vibrations to his body" with a "microwave machine," he ought to have been taken to a psych unit for evaluation. Instead, police told him to avoid the "people" who were bothering him.[3]

Charen reports that due to inadequate treatment of mental illness, one-third of America's homeless people and at least four hundred thousand prison inmates are mentally ill. She also notes that laws can make it difficult or impossible for someone concerned about another person's mental health to get that individual help. She says, "In many states, even if the family members of paranoid schizophrenics beg police and medical authorities to commit someone for short-term evaluation and treatment, civil commitment laws forbid it."[4]

Forced Institutionalization?

Some people suggest that such laws need to change. For example, in the aftermath of the Navy Yard shooting, Fox News reporter Martha MacCallum suggested that certain kinds of mentally ill people need to be locked up regardless of whether they have committed a crime or threatened to commit a crime. She states: "Have we not become so PC [politically correct] that we do not understand that there are categories of people, many people who do not deserve to be institutionalized, but some do."[5]

MacCallum does not state exactly which types of mental ill-

"We have betrayed the mentally ill by drastically reducing the availability of treatment."[3]

— Mona Charen, a columnist with the *Chicago Sun-Times*.

ness warrant automatic institutionalization; there are many such illnesses, ranging from depression to schizophrenia (which can cause breaks from reality, including hallucinations). Nonetheless, an editorial in *USA Today* reminds people such as MacCallum that it would have been illegal to institutionalize the Navy Yard shooter, no matter what kind of mental illness he might have had: "Until the 1970s, snatching people with symptoms off the street and committing them to an institution was permissible. So was keeping them there, no matter their mental state. But a string of court decisions changed the rules by recognizing that the mentally ill have civil rights, and by requiring strong evidence of imminent danger to themselves or others before they can be committed against their will."[6]

Other Violent Offenders

Some people argue that these laws must change because unless more is done to get people with mental illnesses the treatment they need, tragedies like the Navy Yard shooting will continue to occur. But others counter that such extreme measures are unnecessary because studies have shown that only a small percentage of people with a serious mental illness are violent. For example, studies by Jeffrey Swanson, a psychiatry professor at Duke University, have shown that only 7 percent of people with a serious mental illness commit acts of violence. However, Swanson notes, this is still higher than the rate among people who do not have a serious mental illness, which is 2 percent.

Moreover, experts note that it is extremely difficult to predict which mentally ill individuals among those with violent tendencies will actually act on those tendencies. Psychiatrist Marvin Swartz, who served on an American Psychiatric Association Work Group on Violence Risk in 2012, says, "While psychiatrists can often identify circumstances associated with an increased likelihood of violent behavior, they cannot predict dangerousness with definitive accuracy."[7] In fact, Alec Buchanan, an associate professor of psychiatry at Yale University, argues that the only way to have even

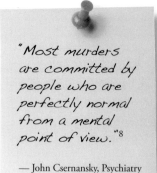

"Most murders are committed by people who are perfectly normal from a mental point of view."[8]

— John Csernansky, Psychiatry Department chairman at Northwestern University.

a slight chance of preventing one mentally ill person from committing an act of violence would be to lock up five to ten of them.

Of course, this approach would do nothing to stop killings by people who are not mentally ill, and as John Csernansky, Psychiatry Department chairman at Northwestern University, reports, "Most murders are committed by people who are perfectly normal from a mental point of view."[8] In fact, *National Journal* reporter Margo Sanger-Katz says:

> Researchers estimate that if mental illness could be eliminated as a factor in violent crime, the overall rate would be reduced by only 4 percent. That means 96 percent of violent crimes—defined by the FBI as murders, robberies, rapes, and aggravated assaults—are committed by people without any mental-health problems at all. Solutions that focus on reducing crimes by the mentally ill will make only a small dent in the nation's rate of gun-related murders, ranging from mass killings to shootings that claim a single victim.[9]

Nonetheless, in recent years the media has paid far more attention to mass shootings than to most other kinds of murders, and the majority of the shooters in these prominent cases have been mentally ill. Therefore mental health issues are at the forefront in discussions on how to reduce America's violence, but there is little agreement on how to balance the needs and rights of people with a mental illness with the needs and rights of those who do not have a mental illness.

Facts

- The *New York Times* reports that out of one hundred shooting rampages that took place between 1949 and 1999, at least half were committed by someone who had shown signs of serious mental illness prior to the shooting.

- In examining sixty-two mass shootings, *Mother Jones* magazine determined that more than half (thirty-six) ended with the perpetrator committing suicide.

- According to Pennsylvania congressman Tim Murphy in a September 19, 2013, report to Congress, the number of beds available for mentally ill patients in psychiatric facilities has gone from five hundred thousand in 1955 to forty thousand today.

- Congressman Tim Murphy reports that only about 2 million of the roughly 11 million Americans with a serious mental illness are receiving treatment for their illness.

- Experts have determined that people with mental illnesses commit at least one thousand homicides each year.

What Are the Origins of Concerns About Mental Illness and Crime?

In the 1970s California experienced a rash of well-publicized murders committed by mentally ill people recently released from mental institutions. For example, roughly three months after being hospitalized three times and then released each time without follow-up treatment, a man was urged by voices in his head to kill thirteen people. Another man killed his wife, three children, and himself just two weeks after being released from a state hospital. In a third case, a person who had been hospitalized five years earlier for paranoid schizophrenia but was no longer receiving treatment for it killed seven people at California State University in Fullerton because he believed everyone was out to kill him.

These individuals had been released as part of a movement called deinstitutionalization, whereby the government sought to move mentally ill people out of mental institutions—also called mental hospitals or lunatic or insane asylums—and into the community. It was largely because of deinstitutionalization that con-

Labeled Hostile

One of the leading advocates for the rights of mental patients is James B. Gottstein, an attorney who learned the importance of such rights firsthand. In June 1982, while suffering from severe sleep deprivation, he had a psychotic episode during which he ran though his neighborhood imagining a devil was after him. Police took him to a mental hospital, where for a month he was forcibly medicated for illnesses he did not have, unable to make people believe he was mentally competent under normal circumstances. Of this experience he says, "When you become a psychiatric patient . . . everything that you do or say can be labeled as a psychiatric symptom. If police knock down your door and haul you off and you get upset, you get labeled as 'hostile' and 'labile.' . . . If you think something is funny and you laugh to yourself, then they write down 'responding to internal stimuli.'" Consequently, he feels fortunate that a doctor finally realized what had caused his psychotic episode, and since then he has fought for a patient's right to refuse psychiatric medicines and for limiting the conditions under which someone can be involuntarily committed.

Quoted in David Brown, "Predicting Violence Is a Work in Progress," *Washington Post*, January 3, 2013. www.washingtonpost.com.

cerns about the impact that mental illness had on crime came to the attention of the national media. However, the public's fears about the dangers of allowing the mentally ill to mingle with the sane had existed for far longer, which is one reason that people with a mental illness had been isolated in mental institutions ever since the mid-1800s.

As an example of how these fears developed, someone who lived near the Rockland County Mental Institution in New York recalls:

"My first memory of Rockland . . . was of hearing my parents talking about a 'lunatic' who had just escaped from the hospital. I didn't know what a lunatic was at 6 or 7 years old, but I could tell by the way they acted that I should be scared. My mother eventually used that fear to keep me in line by saying 'you better be good or the lunatic will get you.' My ears still go up when I hear that word."[10]

Institutional Abuses

Despite such fears, by the 1960s deinstitutionalization had gained many supporters for three reasons. First, the development of medications to treat mental illnesses made it possible for patients to be medically treated at home or at an outpatient clinic. Second, state-run mental institutions were expensive to operate. Third, the abuse of patients was common at many institutions, as were abuses related to the way people were committed to these facilities.

Some of the patients in such places were truly mentally ill, but others had been involuntarily committed by relatives unhappy with their behavior. Relatively little proof of mental problems was required to get a person committed, and once people were deemed insane, they lost all control over their destinies. They could be released from an institution only when one of its doctors deemed them cured, and while institutionalized they might be subjected to cruel treatment. For example, a former patient at the Rockland asylum says:

> I was institutionalized . . . when I was 8 years old (1965–69). . . . I lived in a big dormitory with 50+ children. We were lined up at shower time and lined up to go to cafeteria. I remember spending most of the day in a "day room"—most of the other kids were severely disturbed. . . . If I didn't do as told, they would put me in an isolation room (all day). Once they tied me to a bed with wet sheets layered with ice and opened the window in winter. There was an outside play area where one of the "minders" would hit kids with a wiffle ball bat.[11]

Restricting people's movements by tying them to beds or putting them into straitjackets was a standard way to control patients

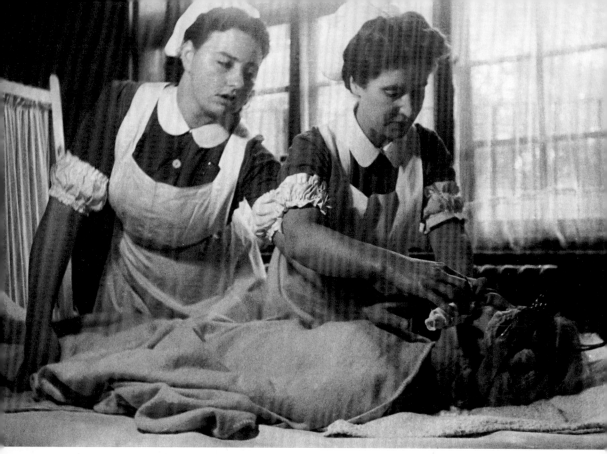

Nurses at a psychiatric hospital prepare a patient for electric shock therapy in 1946. The patient suffered from severe depression, a mental illness once commonly treated this way.

in many asylums. Other common practices were electroconvulsive therapy (shocking patients with electricity), putting people into comas, and performing a type of brain surgery known as a lobotomy. These procedures were intended to be treatments and possibly cures for mental illness, but they often left patients severely damaged. Similarly, beginning in the 1950s patients were treated with powerful psychiatric drugs that often left them acting like zombies, and in crowded facilities these drugs were often administered as a means to control difficult patients, even if their mental problems were minor.

Attempts at Reform

Given such practices, life in asylums was typically bleak and depressing, consisting largely of inadequate treatment and isolation, and patients who complained about their plight were often treated worse than those who suffered in silence. In addition, the loved ones of those in mental institutions were discouraged from contacting them, which only deepened patients' isolation. Family members called on their government representatives to do something about this situation, and in 1963 President John F. Kennedy signed the Community Mental Health Act (CMHA) into law. Its purpose, he said, was to ensure that the "cold mercy of custodial care would be replaced by the open warmth of community."[12]

The CMHA provided grants to states so that they could replace a system of large state-run institutions with small, local community mental health centers. This would enable mental patients who did not pose a clear danger to themselves or others to be released and treated as outpatients in their local communities while they were living at home and, if well enough, holding jobs. But only half of the centers proposed under the law were ever built, and there was often not enough money to meet the needs of those centers that did open. Meanwhile the states began closing the institutions whose services were intended to be replaced by community centers. This led to a reduction in treatment options for people with a mental illness, and those who could not live with family members often became homeless. Left unsupervised, many also failed to take any medications that had been prescribed for them to treat their illness.

Dismantling Public Health Care

The mental health system was further weakened under the presidency of Ronald Reagan in the 1980s. A month before Reagan took office, President Jimmy Carter had increased funding to the mental health system via the Mental Health Systems Act of 1980, which funded federal community centers, but Reagan rescinded this law after his inauguration. Reagan had also been the driving force behind dismantling the mental health system in California while he was governor of the state from 1967 to 1975. During his first year in office he signed a law that eliminated involuntary hospitalizations for mental illness for all but the most extreme cases and made it difficult for a person who had been released from a state mental hospital to be readmitted for another round of treatment.

In supporting such laws, Reagan was acting on beliefs related to economics. He felt that the government should not be spending money to help people with a mental illness; instead, their treatment should be the responsibility of the private sector. Consequently patients who could not live on their own were increasingly housed in for-profit, board-and-care facilities, which meant that they and

A Shocking Event

Americans were first introduced to the horrors of a mass shooting at a school on August 1, 1966, when a gunman opened fire at students at the University of Texas in Austin from the top of an observation tower. The shooter was former marine Charles Whitman, a student at the university, whose ninety-minute rampage—which ended only when the police stormed the twenty-eighth-floor observation deck and killed him—resulted in the deaths of sixteen people and an unborn baby and wounded another thirty-two people. He had also killed his wife and mother at their homes just prior to the shooting. His weapons included rifles, pistols, and a shotgun.

A few months before the massacre, Whitman had visited a psychiatrist at the University Health Center and told him that he had fantasized about shooting people from the tower, but the doctor did not believe Whitman really intended to do so. There is also evidence that Whitman often suffered from sleep deprivation due to combining work and school, and he was taking an amphetamine (a drug that is an addictive stimulant) in order to keep himself going. These conditions might have contributed to his actions on the day of the massacre. However, an autopsy on Whitman's body revealed that he had a small tumor in his brain, and some have suggested that this might have been the reason for his mental problems.

their families, rather than the state, had to pay for their care. Mentally ill people who did not have health insurance or enough funds to pay for treatment on their own often went untreated.

According to E. Fuller Torrey, executive director of the Stanley Medical Research Institute in Chevy Chase, Maryland, and professor of psychiatry at the Uniformed Services University of the Health Sciences, the result of this system was that "by 1975 board-and-care homes had become big business in California," with many of the homes being owned by a few large companies. Patients who could not pay their board-and-care bills were turned out onto the streets. As a result, Torrey reports, "California was the first state to witness not only an increase in homelessness associated with deinstitutionalization but also an increase in incarceration and episodes of violence."[13] The board-and-care approach to deinstitutionalization spread to other states, which then experienced such increases as well—by the middle of the 1970s, in some states the mentally ill accounted for 5 percent of the jail population.

Growing Problems

Nonetheless, deinstitutionalization continued to spread, and in the early 1980s so many state-run hospitals were shut down throughout the country that the number of seriously ill mental patients released onto the streets swelled dramatically. The decade also saw numerous acts of violence throughout the country committed by the mentally ill homeless, sometimes even after their illness had come to the attention of medical professionals. For example, in 1985 a Pennsylvania woman who had been hospitalized twelve times for symptoms of schizophrenia killed three people and wounded seven others in a shopping mall, and a Wisconsin man who had been hospitalized seven times for schizophrenia killed three people in a Catholic church.

During this same period, studies indicated that as many as one-third of all homeless people in the United States were severely mentally ill, and that same year experts estimated that more than one hundred thousand people with serious mental illnesses were in prison. Studies also showed that abuses of mental patients at board-and-care facilities were on the rise. As such problems in-

A homeless person sleeps on a city sidewalk, his possessions piled in a shopping cart beside him. After state-run hospitals were shut down in the 1980s, many patients with mental illness ended up homeless on the streets.

creased, the media began to report on the flaws of deinstitutionalization, telling stories not only of patient abuse but of how difficult life was for mentally ill people living on the streets.

One case that gained a lot of media attention was that of Joyce Brown, who lived on a steam grate at the corner of two streets in New York. Brown had once been a secretary, but after being hospitalized briefly for a mental illness she was no longer able to function in society. She also displayed erratic behavior while living on the street and sometimes darted in front of cars. As a result, the mayor of New York, Ed Koch, had police take her to a hospital against her will, an action that led to legal actions that established that Koch had violated Brown's civil rights. Along with deinstitutionalization had come changes in laws related to commitment, making it very difficult to have someone held involuntarily in a mental institution.

Mass Shootings

Despite concerns about the civil rights of people with mental illnesses, Americans often questioned the wisdom of allowing seriously disturbed individuals to live on the streets. Debates regarding this approach intensified each time a mass shooting occurred because, according to Grant Duwe, a criminologist with the Minnesota Department of Corrections, "Mass shootings provoke instant debates about violence and guns and mental health."[14] An expert on mass murders in the United States, Duwe reports that there were one hundred mass shootings from the 1980s through the 2000s.

The two deadliest events of this period were the San Ysidro McDonald's massacre of 1984 and the Virginia Tech massacre of 2007. The perpetrator of the San Ysidro, California, shooting, James Oliver Huberty, walked into a McDonald's with three weapons—a semi-automatic assault rifle, a pump-action shotgun, and a pistol—as well as bullets able to pierce the kind of body armor worn by police. He then fired 257 rounds of ammunition during an attack and standoff that lasted seventy-seven minutes, killing sixteen adults and five children and injuring nineteen others before a police sniper on the roof of a nearby building managed to shoot and kill him. Investigators subsequently learned that the day before the massacre Huberty had called and left a message with a mental health center saying he needed assistance, but he did not specify his problem, and no one returned his call. On the morning of the massacre he took his family to a zoo, then ate with them at a McDonald's, then went home but later left after telling his wife he was going out to hunt humans. Later she could provide no explanation to police as to why she was not concerned about this remark or her husband's mental health.

The shooter in the Virginia Tech massacre, twenty-three-year-old Seung-Hui Cho, also had mental health issues. An undergraduate student at the Virginia Polytechnic Institute and State University in Blacksburg, Virginia, Cho had been in therapy in middle school and high school for severe depression and other problems.

"Mass shootings provoke instant debates about violence and guns and mental health."[14]

— Grant Duwe, a criminologist with the Minnesota Department of Corrections.

In college he exhibited what professors called disturbing behaviors and was accused of stalking female students. Consequently, in 2005 a Virginia special justice (someone who handles commitment hearings) declared him mentally ill and ordered him to receive treatment as an outpatient. Nonetheless, Cho's mental condition continued to deteriorate, and in April 2007, during his senior year, he engaged in two shooting attacks on campus, one in a residence hall and the other in a classroom building. In between these attacks, which took place two hours apart, he went to his dorm to change out of his bloody clothes. He then went to a nearby post office to mail a package to a news station that contained writings and videotapes in which he attempted to justify his actions and compared himself to Jesus Christ. The second attack ended when he committed suicide after killing thirty-two people and wounding seventeen others.

Changes in Laws

Both of these mass shootings led to changes in federal gun laws. The San Ysidro massacre brought forth a ban on the kind of armor-piercing bullets the gunman used. The Virginia Tech massacre resulted in a law that expanded the system for checking the background of someone wanting to purchase a firearm, with the aim of preventing those legally declared mentally ill from owning a gun. The Virginia Tech incident also led the state of Virginia to improve its approach to commitment decisions by making it easier for the mental health system and the judicial system to work together to identify and monitor the treatment of seriously ill individuals like Cho.

However, little was done to address the serious problems of the mental health system as a whole, and this was true after subsequent mass shootings as well. In fact, experts have complained that each time a mass shooting is committed by a mentally ill individual, there are many impassioned calls for reform that ultimately lead to nothing. For example, John Harris, clinical assistant professor of medicine at the University of Arizona College of Medicine, says,

"Rampage violence seems to lead to repeated cycles of anguish, investigation, recrimination, and heated debate, with little real progress in prevention. These types of events can lead to despair about their inevitability and unpredictability."[15]

Studies have shown that such events can also lead people to assume that someone who is mentally ill is likely to be violent, although that is not the case. Indeed, an Indiana University study found that between 1950 and 1996 the number of Americans who associated mental illness with dangerous, violent behavior had almost doubled. A Gallup poll taken in September 2013 found that 48 percent of Americans put the most blame for gun violence on mental illness.

The Sandy Hook Shooting

The same poll, which was taken in the aftermath of the Navy Yard shooting committed by Aaron Alexis that killed twelve, found that the number of people blaming easy access to guns for gun violence had dropped 6 points, to 40 percent, since 2011, when a similar poll was taken in the aftermath of the shooting of a congresswoman by a mentally ill man at a political event in Arizona. Largely responsible for this drop was a mass shooting in Newtown, Connecticut, that ignited passions related to the issue of gun control. Opponents of gun control used this tragedy as a means to focus the blame for gun violence squarely on people with mental illnesses. For example, at a press conference after the shooting, the executive vice president of the National Rifle Association (NRA), Wayne LaPierre, said, "We have a completely cracked mentally ill system that's got these monsters walking the streets,"[16] and a gun owner protesting gun control outside Connecticut's state capital subsequently told a reporter, "We don't go around shooting people, the sick people do. They need to be fixed."[17]

The "monster" that LaPierre was referring to was twenty-year-old Adam Lanza, who in December 2012 shot and killed his mother before going to Sandy Hook Elementary School and killing twenty children—all between the ages of six and seven—and six adults there before killing himself. Investigators later deter-

"Their first step in becoming criminals was getting their hands on guns and ammunition."[18]

— Convicted felon Matthew Parker, in speaking of mass shooters.

mined that he had brought with him a semi-automatic rifle, two semi-automatic handguns, and enough ammunition to kill all 450 children at the school if police had not interrupted him. They also learned that Lanza did not speak during the shooting and shot every victim more than once—one six-year-old boy was shot eleven times.

After the massacre investigators went to Lanza's home and found more weapons, including two rifles, more than a half-dozen knives, three samurai swords, and sixteen hundred rounds of ammunition. They were unable to access his computer to see whether he had left behind any disturbing writings because Lanza had intentionally damaged it before embarking on his killing spree. However, investigators did determine that Lanza's mother had been worried about her son's mental health and might have been planning to have him committed to a mental health facility. Despite this, she had supported his interest in guns and often took him to a shooting range.

Gun control advocates blame the prevalence of guns in the Lanza household for the Sandy Hook shooting. They say that without access to guns, the young man would have been unable to act on his violent impulses, regardless of the reason for those impulses. As Matthew Parker, a convicted felon who has served time in a state prison, notes in considering the kind of people who commit violent acts like Lanza's, "It's plain to see that you're dealing with sick individuals whose criminal proclivities existed solely in their minds. Their first step in becoming criminals was getting their hands on guns and ammunition."[18]

Nonetheless, the NRA has fought against any changes to gun laws while continuing to argue for changes to the mental health laws. LaPierre has also accused government leaders of not wanting to fix the mental health system. He says: "They've emptied the institutions and every police officer knows dangerous people out there on the streets right now. They shouldn't be on the streets, they've stopped taking their medicine and yet they're out there walking around."[19] Such remarks have served to ratchet up Americans' fears about people with mental illnesses.

"They've emptied the institutions and every police officer knows dangerous people out there on the streets right now."[19]

— Wayne LaPierre of the National Rifle Association (NRA), in complaining about inaction by government leaders.

Facts

- A national survey by the Substance Abuse and Mental Health Services Administration (SAMHSA) revealed that over 29 percent of Americans fail to seek treatment for mental health problems because they fear being institutionalized and/or stigmatized because of their illness.

- *Mother Jones* magazine reports that the largest reduction in mental health funding since deinstitutionalization occurred in 2009 when, due to an economic recession, US states cut $4.35 billion in public mental health spending, with the money to be reduced over a period of three years.

- *Mother Jones* magazine reports that in 2013 there were forty-three thousand psychiatric beds in the United States, or about fourteen beds per hundred thousand people, which is the same ratio as in the year 1850.

- According to the World Health Organization (WHO), roughly 20 percent of children and adolescents throughout the world have mental disorders or problems.

- WHO reports that poor countries have only 0.05 psychiatrists per hundred thousand people, whereas wealthy countries such as the United States have rates roughly 170 times higher.

- The Center for American Progress, a Washington, DC, think tank, has estimated that the mass shooting at Virginia Tech cost taxpayers $48.2 million because of expenses related to the work done by police, investigators, hospital and university personnel, litigators, and others.

CHAPTER TWO

How Strong Is the Link Between Mental Illness and Crime?

On January 8, 2011, US representative Gabrielle "Gabby" Giffords was meeting with constituents in a grocery store parking lot just outside of Tucson, Arizona. There were about thirty people present when a man pulled out a gun and shot Giffords in the head, then continued firing at bystanders. She survived, but six others were killed and an additional thirteen injured before members of the crowd subdued the shooter. A fourteenth person was injured while tackling the gunman.

The killer was twenty-two-year-old Jared Lee Loughner, who just a few months earlier had been suspended from his community college because he was exhibiting disturbing behavior and had been caught carrying a knife. Before this suspension, one of his classmates had written to friends that Loughner was a "mentally unstable person . . . that scares the living crap out of me. He is one of those whose picture you see on the news, after he has come into class with an automatic weapon."[20] Loughner also disrupted classes, which led several teachers and students to complain about him to the administration. Consequently, the condition of allowing him to return to class after his suspension was that he receive a mental health evaluation. Rather than do so, however, Loughner dropped out of school.

A Paranoid Schizophrenic

After the shooting, investigators learned that Loughner had been posting rambling antigovernment writings and videos online. In some of them he claimed that the government was trying to control people's minds through their language. He had also met Giffords in 2007 at another event for constituents and become obsessed with her. In addition, a psychiatrist had noted in 2006 that Loughner was displaying symptoms of schizophrenia. However, he was not officially diagnosed with the disorder until shortly before his trial, and he was subsequently sentenced to life in prison.

Most experts believe that Loughner has a particular type of schizophrenia known as paranoid schizophrenia. Paranoia is a mental condition involving delusions arising from the idea that people are out to harm the sufferer. Schizophrenia is a mental disorder involving false perceptions, inappropriate actions and feelings, scattered thoughts, a withdrawal from reality, fantasies, and hallucinations. E. Fuller Torrey calls Loughner "a textbook case" of paranoid schizophrenia, saying:

> "If . . . you have paranoid delusions and you become convinced that the woman who lives across the street is sending signals into your brain, then you may try to hurt her first."[22]
>
> — Psychiatrist E. Fuller Torrey.

> Most psychiatrists will tell you they need to examine a patient before diagnosing him, but this guy has all of the symptoms. He has the right age of onset. He has a deteriorating social course. . . . He has delusions, and they're pretty strange. It's common for schizophrenics to think people are trying to control their mind, but thinking the government is trying to control your grammar—I've never heard that before. The real tip-off is the markedly disorganized speech, which you see in the rambling videos. This is the kind of disorganized speech that you virtually never get in any other condition.[21]

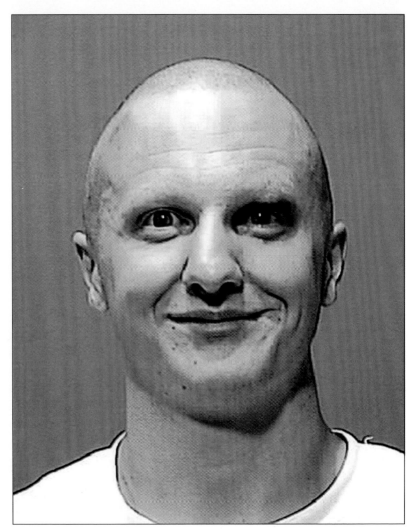

Jared Lee Loughner, who killed six people and injured more than a dozen others in Arizona in January 2011, had been suspended from community college after exhibiting disturbing behavior. Experts believe Loughner suffers from paranoid schizophrenia.

Torrey reports that while some schizophrenics can be prone to extreme acts of violence, paranoid schizophrenia is more often the type of schizophrenia to trigger violence. He explains why: "If you have grandiose delusions [caused by other forms of schizophrenia or mental illness]—if you think you're the king of Washington, for instance—you're not likely to kill anyone. If, on the other hand, you have paranoid delusions [consistent with paranoid schizo-phrenia] and you become convinced that the woman who lives across the street is sending signals into your brain, then you may try to hurt her first."[22]

However, Torrey adds that whether a schizophrenic is medicated has a huge bearing on whether he might become violent. He reports:

> There is a very small number of people with schizophrenia who are, indeed, dangerous and do things like this. It's very important to emphasize that the vast majority of people with this disease are not dangerous, and there are certain predictors in terms of who will be dangerous. Past history of violence, substance abuse, both of which are predictors for non-schizophrenics, too. But I've followed schizophrenia for 30 years, and I have never seen one of these high-profile homicides where the fellow hasn't been off his medication when he did it. Being off medication is a clear risk factor for people who have a past history.[23]

Indeed, when Loughner was finally medicated for his illness, his behavior changed. Paul Bright of the *San Francisco Examiner* reports: "Even during his arrest, Loughner was reported to have had a psychotic meltdown, claiming his brain's thoughts were being manipulated by a radio. He was deemed a suicidal risk and was forced to take anti-psychotic meds. Once those took effect, Loughner became compliant with prosecutors and expressed remorse over his actions."[24]

Various studies indicate that on any given day, approximately 50 percent of the roughly 4 million Americans who currently suffer from the two most serious types of mental illness, schizophrenia and bipolar disorder, are not being treated for their illness. Studies also indicate that roughly half the people with these illnesses do not realize that they are ill. Instead, they believe that their hallucinations and delusions are real. As psychiatrist Paul Steinberg explains:

> When the voices [in the sufferer's head] become commands, all bets are off. The commands might insist, for example, that a person jump out of a window, even if he has no intention of dying, or grab a set of guns and kill people, without any sense that he is wreaking havoc. Additional

symptoms include other distorted thinking, like the notion that something—even a spaceship, or a comic book character—is controlling one's thoughts and actions.[25]

Steinberg reports that the reason for this lies in the fact that schizophrenia is associated with biochemical changes in a part of the brain called the frontal cortex, involved in abstract thinking, social behavior, and language. These changes can cause the brain to produce, for example, conversations that only the sufferer can hear.

Media Attention

Beset by imagined voices and other hallucinations, some sufferers turn violent. In some cases this violence is limited to a brief period—an acute psychotic episode involving a temporary delusion or hallucination, for example—and as the symptoms of this episode abate, the violence ends. In other cases the sufferer has a complete and permanent break with reality.

Studies have also indicated that a schizophrenic's violence can fluctuate. This means that someone who is nonviolent might experience temporary flashes of violence. However, when this violence is acted upon it is more likely to be aimed at family members and/or friends and to take place at home.

Nonetheless, sensational killings gain most of the media attention when it comes to violence committed by people with a mental illness. As John Csernansky notes, this is because the news media tends to report on the unusual and seemingly inexplicable. He says, "If an ordinary person shoots his business partner for money or his wife for infidelity, it doesn't hit the papers in the same way. If a person with schizophrenia commits an act of violence and that is driven by their delusion, it's more than likely going to be an act that doesn't make any sense."[26]

The public's fascination with such stories also drives the entertainment media to use news reports of sensational killers as inspiration in works of fiction. Studies show that whenever a television show, movie, or book features a mentally ill character, that character is 50 to 60 percent more likely to be the perpetrator of a crime and/or to commit an act of violence than to be the victim of a crime

Cultural Influences

Experts say that a person's culture influences the delusions the person will have if he or she develops a psychotic condition. This was first discovered by researchers with the Tokyo Metropolitan College of Allied Medical Sciences, who compared the schizophrenic delusions of patients in the cities of Tokyo, Japan; Vienna, Austria; and Tübingen, Germany. Among all three groups, 80 percent of patients had negative delusions. However, the negative delusions among those in Vienna and Tübingen tended to concern poisoning or religion, whereas in Tokyo the patients' delusions primarily concerned being slandered by others. The researchers concluded that slander was the primary delusion in Japan because the country has a "shame culture" in which someone without honor and integrity is shamed. In reporting on this research, health writer John Cloud of *Time* magazine says, "Such studies suggest that the broader culture—which would include the political climate—could affect the content of a psychotic person's delusions, including what or whom the person perceives as threats."

John Cloud, "The Troubled Life of Jared Loughner," *Time*, January 15, 2011. http://content.time.com.

or an act of violence. Yet as Cheryl K. Olson, codirector of the Center for Mental Health and Media at the Massachusetts General Hospital Department of Psychiatry, says, while "studies have found that dangerousness/crime is the most common theme of stories on mental illness, . . . research suggests that mentally ill people are more likely to be victims than perpetrators of violence."[27]

Olson's position is borne out by one of the most significant studies conducted on the link between mental illness and crime. This study was conducted in 2008 in Sweden, where detailed data are kept regarding how many crimes are committed by the mentally ill. After reviewing data spanning thirteen years, the researchers found that people with severe mental illness are responsible for only one in twenty violent crimes, and 18 percent of murders and attempted murders are committed by people with a mental illness. In fact, only 5.2 percent of all violent crimes over the studied period were committed by people with severe mental illness.

In commenting on these results, a spokesman for the Sainsbury Centre for Mental Health says:

This study shows clearly that people with severe mental health conditions commit a very small proportion of violent crimes and that the widely held prejudices about schizophrenia are inaccurate and unfair. It is now time to stop this stale debate about mental health and violence and start looking at how to overcome the prejudice and consequent discrimination that stop people with severe mental health conditions from having an ordinary life in our society.[28]

Catherine Walker, a writer for the UK website Mental Healthy, says that diagnostic labels contribute to inaccurate views on mental illness and violence. She explains:

When referring to a crime where the perpetrator had a mental illness, it is very easy to define the criminal as his or her diagnosis. For example "paranoid schizophrenic kills inmate" is a headline that is deemed wholly acceptable by most media, however I can now see that running such a headline can be unhelpful. In doing so we are not simply defining two elements of the perpetrator separately, but creating the direct link between diagnosis and crime, as if they were mutually inclusive.[29]

Bipolar Disorder

Nonetheless, researchers use these labels in their studies of the link between mental illness and crime. Schizophrenia has received the most attention in this regard, but bipolar disorder has also been connected to violent and/or criminal behavior. This disorder is a condition whereby a person has alternating periods of depression and periods of being extremely happy or being cross or irritable. According to psychiatrists Allison M.R. Lee and Igor Galynker, both experts on

The Tarasoff Ruling

Although US law acknowledges that psychiatrists are unable to determine with certainty which individuals might act on violent thoughts, it does charge them with the duty of informing a third party of a patient's violent intentions, and it puts them at risk of being held liable if they fail to do this. The judicial decision that established this duty is known as the Tarasoff ruling, named for University of California student Tatiana Tarasoff. In 1969 Tarasoff was stabbed to death by another student, Prosenjit Poddar, who had become obsessed with her after she rejected his amorous advances. At the time, Poddar was displaying symptoms of paranoid schizophrenia, and while being treated at the university's health center he told a psychologist that he planned to kill Tarasoff. The psychologist never notified anyone of this threat, and several months later Poddar carried out his plan in exactly the way he had described it to the psychologist. The victim's family subsequently filed a lawsuit against the regents of the university, and after the case reached the California Supreme Court, the justices decided that mental health professionals whose patients make specific threats of bodily harm against another person or persons must notify police and/or warn the potential victim(s) and/or take other reasonable measures to protect the potential victim(s). Other states soon established "duty to warn" requirements as well.

bipolar disorder, studies have shown that nearly 50 percent of people diagnosed with bipolar disorder have acted violently in the past and are prone to becoming agitated to a degree that makes violence more likely. In part, they say, this is because severe bipolar disorder can be the result of serious psychological trauma during childhood, and this trauma makes the victim more likely to act out.

Violence is even more likely when bipolar disorder occurs in conjunction with schizophrenia. Authorities suspect that twenty-year-old Michael Brandon Hill might have had both conditions. He had previously been diagnosed with bipolar disorder. They think he might also have suffered from schizophrenia on the day he walked into an elementary school near Atlanta, Georgia, in August 2013 carrying an assault rifle and 498 rounds of ammunition. He told a woman in the school office to call a local television station so it could send reporters to cover his shootout with police. It is unclear whether he had brought the ammunition solely for the shootout or whether he was intending to kill schoolchildren as well. However, after the police arrived Hill fired off only six rounds, hitting no one, and then surrendered his weapon. Authorities later discovered that he had recently stopped taking his medication for bipolar disorder and attention deficit disorder (ADD).

Personality Disorders

Personality disorders have also been associated with violent acts. In fact, experts have found that when severe mental illnesses like schizophrenia and bipolar disorder occur in conjunction with a personality disorder, it increases the risk that the sufferer will become violent. According to the guidebook that mental heath professionals use to make their diagnoses, the *Diagnostic and Statistical Manual* (DSM), a personality disorder is an "enduring pattern of inner experience and behavior that deviates markedly from the expectation of the individual's culture, is pervasive and inflexible, has an onset in adolescence or early adulthood, is stable over time, and leads to distress or impairment."[30]

Though not technically a mental disorder, a personality disorder can cause mental distress. This is because sufferers typically have trouble relating to others and to their surroundings, a prob-

lem often associated with a rigidity of thinking that leads them to behave the same way regardless of the situation and believe that their troubles are the fault of the people around them. This attitude can cause the kind of anger and frustration that leads to acting out against others.

Sometimes this acting out can be impulsive, but in many cases it involves controlled planning. Studies have shown that mass murderers, including serial killers (killers who target their victims individually), might plan their murders for days, weeks, or even months before taking action. J. Reid Meloy, a professor of psychiatry at the University of California at San Diego and an expert in mass murderers, says that this is true even when the killer has a severe mental disorder as well as a personality disorder. He explains: "The majority of adult mass murderers are psychotic, meaning they have broken with consensual reality and perceive the world in an idiosyncratic and often paranoid way. Yet they may research

A mother tightly hugs her four-year-old daughter after a shooting at the girl's school in August 2013 near Atlanta, Georgia. The suspected shooter had been diagnosed with bipolar disorder and, authorities said, had stopped taking his medication.

the internet for weapons, practice video games to sharpen their marksmanship, purchase weapons and ammunition, conduct surveillance of the target, and carry out their mass murder, all from within a delusion."[31]

Meloy adds that when mass murderers finally do act they tend to carry out the steps of their plans methodically and seemingly without emotion. He reports, "I have forensically evaluated a number of mass murderers in prison or forensic hospitals, and with few exceptions, there was no evidence of a high state of emotional arousal when the killings occurred. Witnesses who have survived mass murders invariably describe the shooter as cool, calm, and deliberate—a lack of emotion that is a corollary of planned violence."[32] This same coolness can also occur prior to the violent event. As a Harvard Medical School newsletter on mental health warns, in sessions with a psychiatrist someone planning to commit a crime "may be guarded, less emotional, and even thoughtful, thereby masking any signs of violent intent."[33]

Other Factors

Compounding the problem of determining whether someone who is mentally ill is at risk of committing a violent act is the fact that many of these individuals have complex problems and multiple diagnoses. As Meloy explains, "Most are complex in their motivations and psychopathology. They often have both mental and personality disorders . . . [so] when it comes to risk mitigation, fully understanding the range and complexity of these individuals' disturbances is critical." Moreover, he says, this complexity makes it impossible to point to one diagnosis as the reason a mentally ill person has committed murder. In the case of Loughner, for example, Meloy says, "Loughner has given paranoid schizophrenia a bad name—many other factors contributed to his attempted assassination and mass murder."[34]

Indeed, experts have identified many factors that contribute to someone's desire to commit a violent act aside from whether the person has a mental illness. One factor is whether the person is under the influence of

"[Mass shooter Jarod] Loughner has given paranoid schizophrenia a bad name—many other factors contributed to his attempted assassination and mass murder."[34]

— J. Reid Meloy, a professor of psychiatry at the University of California at San Diego.

alcohol or drugs to the point that he or she is incapable of controlling emotions and actions. Other factors are age and gender, since young people are more likely to become violent than older adults, and men are more likely to become violent than women. In fact, according to the Treatment Advocacy Center of Arlington, Virginia, which was founded by Torrey to help people suffering from mental illness, "Being a young male or being a substance abuser (alcohol or drugs) is a greater risk factor for violent behavior than being mentally ill."[35]

Another factor is whether an individual is suffering from lack of sleep. In fact, this might have contributed to the crimes of serial killer David Berkowitz, who shot and killed six people and wounded seven during eight shootings in New York in 1976–1977. Psychiatrists working with police diagnosed him as a paranoid schizophrenic based on his insistence that he killed on the orders of an ancient demon who had taken possession of his neighbor's dog. Later Berkowitz claimed that he had lied about hearing voices in order to plead insanity and avoid jail, but he was still convicted of murder and sentenced to life in prison. However, Virginia physician Nicola Davies believes that Berkowitz's desire to kill might have been partly due to his extreme insomnia, explaining: "Sleep deprivation adversely affects the brain, causing changes in thoughts and behaviours. Extreme sleep deprivation as experienced by Berkowitz can cause confusion, memory lapses, hallucinations, stress, irritability, and even mental illness. So, yes, Berkowitz's lack of sleep is likely to have played a part in his crimes."[36]

People under social stress due to poverty, homelessness, or some other aspect of having a low socioeconomic status are also more likely to become violent, as are people under personal stress due, for example, to unemployment or divorce. Although having a mental illness makes it more likely that someone under stress will become hostile, it is not necessary for a mental illness to be present in order for certain people to "snap" and commit violence.

Nonetheless, the media's reaction to mass shootings and other

"Being a young male or being a substance abuser (alcohol or drugs) is a greater risk factor for violent behavior than being mentally ill."[35]

— Psychiatrist E. Fuller Torrey.

attacks on strangers has produced fears among the general public that anyone who is mentally ill is dangerous. According to the Substance Abuse and Mental Health Services Administration, 61 percent of Americans believe that schizophrenics are highly likely to become violent, and 64 percent would not want to work with a schizophrenic. More than 38 percent would not be friends with anyone who had any kind of mental illness, and more than 68 percent would not want someone suffering from depression to marry a family member.

In commenting on these findings, Gwen Skinner of the Georgia State Division of Mental Health, Developmental Disabilities and Addictive Diseases expresses the view of many mental health professionals when she says, "People should not fear those with mental illness. Most people who suffer from a mental illness are not violent. They are normal human beings experiencing a health problem."[37] But each new report of a shooting committed by someone with a mental illness only reinforces the public's perception that mentally ill people are more prone to violence than those without mental illnesses.

Facts

- According to schizophrenia.com, in the United States approximately two hundred thousand homeless individuals, or one-third of the total homeless population, have schizophrenia or bipolar disorder, based on data from the Department of Health and Human Services.

- The National Institute of Mental Health reports that studies show that people with serious mental illnesses, such as schizophrenia and bipolar disorder, have roughly a 16 percent chance of displaying violent behavior at some point in their lives, whereas those without mental illness diagnoses have only about a 7 percent chance.

- Research reported in the *Psychological Bulletin* in 2009 involving a review of cases from 1990 to 2004 concluded that major mental disorders accounted for 5 to15 percent of community violence.

- As reported in 2009 in the *Annals of Medical Psychology* (Paris), researchers who studied the cases of 210 convicted murderers in Angers, France, found that 20 percent had been diagnosed with a personality disorder.

- Studies have shown that people with psychosis are roughly 50 to 70 percent more likely to commit violence than people with no mental disorders.

CHAPTER THREE

What Role Does Substance Abuse Play in Mental Illness and Crime?

On May 22, 2002, at an airport in Kenner, Louisiana, former marine Patrick Gott reached into a large bag, pulled out a shotgun, and aimed it at people standing in front of the Southwest Airlines ticket counter. He then shot a traveler from California in the stomach, fatally wounding her. He was about to fire at others when three bystanders tackled him to the ground.

Shortly after his arrest doctors determined that Gott had been suffering from delusional paranoia and depression at the time of the shooting, and they subsequently expanded their diagnosis to include schizophrenia. Therefore, although he was charged with second-degree murder, he was deemed unfit to stand trial, and a court declared him not guilty by reason of insanity. He was then sent to a maximum-security state hospital, where he was medicated for his mental illnesses.

In May 2012 Gott was declared "completely, 100-percent non-symptomatic"[38] and transferred to a less secure hospital. The following year he asked for but was refused permission to occasionally leave the hospital on supervised day trips offered for certain patients. His goal, he said, was ultimately to leave the hospital permanently. "I want to get back to the free world, the real world,"[39] he told the judge who ruled on his request. Gott expressed remorse for the killing but blamed it not only on his mental illnesses but on his problems with substance abuse. Prior to the shooting he had been a heavy user of marijuana, cocaine, and alcohol, and in the midst of his addictions he became paranoid. He stopped drinking tap water, convinced it would poison him, and after he started hearing knocks on his door when no one was there, he was sure someone was trying to drive him crazy. Gott told the judge that because of this he would never abuse drugs or alcohol again, but others expressed concerns that he would be unable to maintain his resolve if released into the community.

Increasing Hostility

Experts say that the abuse of drugs and/or alcohol can make many people, mentally ill or not, more hostile. Carolyn Anderson of the Gulf Coast Substance Abuse Task Force, located in Mississippi, explains, "Alcohol and drug addiction actually changes a person's personal characteristics where they may have been sweet, they may have been involved in their family, and suddenly they're argumentative. It's like they have a grudge on their shoulder."[40] She reports that US government statistics indicate that 70 percent of all murders in America are committed by someone who is under the influence of alcohol, drugs, or both.

Studies have also shown that the negative effects of drugs and/or alcohol can be even more pronounced in the mentally ill. According to a Harvard Medical School newsletter on mental health, "these substances simultaneously impair judgment, change a person's emotional equilibrium, and remove cognitive inhibitions. In people with psychiatric disorders, substance abuse may exacerbate symptoms such as paranoia, grandiosity, or hostility. Patients who abuse drugs or alcohol are also less likely to adhere to treatment for a mental illness, and that can worsen psychiatric symptoms."[41]

"Patients who abuse drugs or alcohol are . . . less likely to adhere to treatment for a mental illness, and that can worsen psychiatric symptoms."[41]

— Harvard Medical School newsletter on mental health.

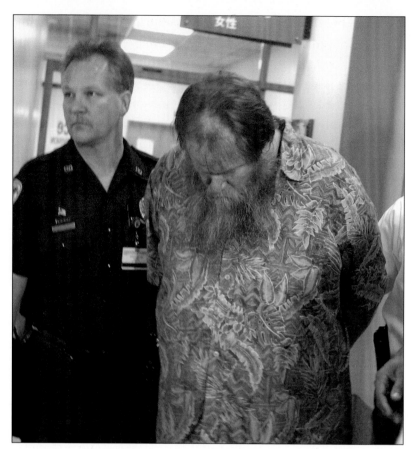

A police officer escorts Patrick Gott out of the airport in Kenner, Louisiana, after he shot and killed one person. Authorities said Gott suffered from mental illness in addition to being a heavy drug user.

In fact, studies by forensic psychiatrist Seena Fazel of Oxford University have shown that whereas the rate of violence for schizophrenics without a substance abuse disorder is 8.5 percent and for bipolar individuals without a substance abuse disorder is 4.9 percent, with a substance abuse disorder the rate of violence for these two types of people is 27.6 percent and 21.3 percent, respectively. Another study, the MacArthur Violence Risk Assessment Study reported in 2011, found that 31 percent of people who had a dual diagnosis of both a substance abuse disorder and a psychiatric disorder committed at least one act of violence in a year, compared with 18 percent of people who had only a psychiatric disorder.

Masking Mental Illness

Family members of murderers often say, in the days after the crime, that their loved one seemed like a different person while under the influence of drugs or alcohol. For example, Mindy McDonald, whose twenty-nine-year-old son-in-law Ryan Abeyta strangled his mother to death in 2011 at her home in Gulfport, Mississippi, and then dumped her body in some nearby woods, blamed the murder on his addiction. "It was the alcohol. It was this thing that just took over. It really did. And drugs took over. It really did and made him someone he wasn't."[42]

Indeed, during his murder trial Abeyta testified that prior to the killing—which occurred during a fight over his mother's accusation that he had taken her debit card—he had injected himself with cocaine and had a conversation with the devil, a remark reminiscent of schizophrenic David Berkowitz's claim that a demon had urged him to kill. But Abeyta never claimed to have a mental illness, only an addiction, and a jury convicted him of murder after only two days of testimony and thirty-five minutes of deliberation; he was then sentenced to life in prison.

While Abeyta was never diagnosed with a mental illness, experts say that sometimes a drug and/or alcohol problem can mask mental problems and leave them undiagnosed. Indeed, mental illness and substance abuse often go hand in hand. According to New York University psychiatrist Stephen Gilman, who specializes in addiction issues, "Fifty percent of those with an addictive disorder will have a psychiatric disorder. And for those who have a psychiatric disorder, about 20 percent have an addiction problem."[43]

James Garbutt, professor of psychiatry at the University of North Carolina at Chapel Hill, suggests that these percentages are higher when it comes to certain kinds of disorders. Specifically, he says, "A variety of mental illnesses such as post-traumatic stress disorder, antisocial personality disorder [characterized by a lack of empathy toward other people], anxiety, sleep disorders, or depression, increase the risk of addiction. Those with the highest risk of addiction have bipolar disorder or schizophrenia—up to 50 percent [of people with these conditions] can have an addiction."[44]

The reason that addiction and mental illness are often seen together, he explains, is because drugs and alcohol can alter the psychological effects of certain disorders. For example, drugs or alcohol can lessen the anxiety and agitation that a schizophrenic

Violence as a Side Effect

In the aftermath of a mass shooting in Texas at the Fort Hood military base in 2009 that resulted in thirteen deaths, the media assumed that the reason for this massacre was political and/or religious. This was because the perpetrator, Nidal Malik Hasan, was a Muslim who had e-mailed an anti-American cleric in Yemen. Yet there was not enough evidence surrounding this connection to lead the government to declare the massacre an act of terrorism, and some of Hasan's behavior and comments leading up to his trial in a military court led a few people to suspect mental problems were behind his attack. In support of this theory, they pointed to the fact that Hasan was a psychiatrist with access to antidepressant drugs, and many mass shooters had been taking such drugs at the time of their attacks.

No studies have yet proved a cause-and-effect relationship between antidepressants and violent acts against others, although many studies have shown that these drugs can greatly increase the risk of suicide. Nonetheless, courts have begun to recognize that antidepressants can provide a motive for murder, as evidenced by the fact that in 2012 a Canadian judge ruled that a fifteen-year-old boy killed his friend as a direct result of taking Prozac. During Hasan's trial, however, the government did not bring up his mental health, nor did Hasan—who insisted on acting as his own attorney—and he was found guilty in August 2013 and sentenced to death.

experiences as a result of hallucinations and delusions, and alcohol can lessen the extremes of the mood swings experienced by someone with bipolar disorder. Therefore some mentally ill people use these substances as an intentional or instinctive form of self-medication that can lead to serious addictions.

Cocaine and Heroin

Not all drugs produce the same responses, however, and even the same drug can produce different responses in different individuals. Still, one drug is consistently associated with psychiatric disorders: cocaine. Cocaine is a stimulant and a pain blocker that also raises levels of dopamine in the brain. (Dopamine is associated with a person's ability to experience pleasure.) By doing so, the drug changes the way its user thinks and feels.

Studies have shown that more than two-thirds of cocaine users suffer from paranoia and depression, and those who have one of these disorders prior to using the drug will typically see these conditions worsen. Cocaine can also cause hallucinations, delusions, mood disorders, anxiety disorders, and sleep disorders. In schizophrenics the drug causes a serious increase in symptoms of mania and psychosis and dramatically increases the risk of the user committing impulsive and violent acts.

Another drug associated with serious mental illness is heroin. This drug is a depressant that slows down the central nervous system and the way it communicates with the brain. People with anxiety and agitation are especially drawn to this drug because it calms them down. In addition, some schizophrenics find that heroin lessens their psychotic symptoms, especially delusions and auditory hallucinations. However, if they stop using the drug their symptoms typically come back worse than before.

Causing Illnesses

Sometimes substance abuse can actually cause a mental illness. According to the National Alliance on Mental Illness (NAMI): "Drugs and alcohol can cause a person without mental illness to experience the onset of symptoms for the first time. For example, a twenty-year-old college student who begins to hear threatening voices inside of his head and becomes paranoid that his chemistry professor is poisoning his food after smoking marijuana could represent a reaction to the drug (potentially called a "substance-induced psychosis") or the first episode of psychosis for this individual."[45]

An example of an illegal drug that causes mental disorders is MDMA (3,4-methylenedioxymethamphetamine), commonly known as ecstasy. Long periods of use so deplete the levels of serotonin in the brain that it causes depression, anxiety, and other disorders. In addition, in young people it can interfere with certain aspects of brain development, causing problems with social skills and cognition.

Chronic alcohol abuse can also bring on mental disorders. A depressant, alcohol alters the brain chemistry in ways that make people less anxious and less inhibited. This is why people with anxiety disorders tend to self-medicate with alcohol. However, the more alcohol a person consumes, the more of the brain is affected, and this can result in a flood of negative emotions that include anger, aggression, and depression.

Ironically, chronic abuse can also heighten the very anxiety that the alcohol was meant to curb. This occurs for two reasons. First, heavy drinking can change the way the brain takes in information, making it hone in on one single aspect of the environment rather than absorb circumstances as a whole. This means, for example, that during a conversation an alcoholic might hear only a negative, anxiety-provoking comment in the midst of a flurry of positive comments. Second, chronic alcoholism reduces the amount of serotonin in the brain, making it harder for the alcoholic to maintain a positive mood. Consequently, alcoholics have an increased risk of suffering from severe depression and suicidal thinking, as do people who abuse drugs that lower serotonin.

Studies have shown that approximately 90 percent of all individuals who committed suicide had one or more diagnosable psychiatric conditions, including severe depression, bipolar disorder, and schizophrenia. Studies have also shown that suicidal substance abusers are also more likely to commit violent acts. According to clinical psychologist Mark Ilgen and research health science specialist Felicia Kleinberg, "Up to 75% of those who begin addiction treatment report having engaged in violent behavior (eg, physical assault, mugging, attacking others with a weapon)." They also

"Drugs and alcohol can cause a person without mental illness to experience the onset of symptoms for the first time."[45]

— National Alliance on Mental Illness.

The Addiction Equals Disease Controversy

The most recent versions of the *Diagnostic and Statistical Manual of Mental Disorders* (DSM), the guidebook that provides standard criteria by which mental health professionals diagnose diseases and disorders, classifies addictions to alcohol and/or drugs as psychiatric disorders. However, Nora Volkow, director of the National Institute on Drug Abuse, points out that many people are unaware of this classification, and she says that in order to be successful in dealing with substance abuse issues "we need to first recognize that drug addiction is a mental illness." Her organization has also called drug addiction a brain disease.

But others are opposed to labeling substance addictions as mental illnesses or brain diseases. For example, Marc Lewis, a developmental neuroscientist and professor of developmental psychology, insists that the "disease model" for addiction is wrong because it does not explain the reason that many addicts eliminate their addictions on their own. He says, "True, you get spontaneous recovery with medical diseases, but not very often, especially with serious ones. Yet many if not most addicts get better by themselves, without medically prescribed treatment . . . and often after leaving inadequate treatment programs and getting more creative with their personal issues." Therefore he views addiction "as *an extreme form of normality*, if one can say such a thing. Perhaps more precisely: *an extreme form of learning*. No doubt addiction is a frightening, often horrible, state to endure, whether in oneself or in one's loved ones. But that doesn't make it a disease."

Quoted in Scott Kellogg and Andrew Tatarsky, "Addiction Is a Mental Illness—Treat It That Way," AlterNet, March 3, 2013. www.alternet.org.

Marc Lewis, "Why Addiction Is NOT a Brain Disease," Public Library of Science (PLoS) blog, November 12, 2012. http://blogs.plos.org.

report that studies suggest "individuals who have difficulty in controlling their anger may be more likely to act impulsively, thus turning the violence on themselves rather than on others."[46]

However, sometimes in their desire to kill themselves they risk killing others. This is true in circumstances commonly known as suicide by cop, whereby someone commits a violent crime—such as a mass shooting—in the hope that when police arrive at the scene there will be a shootout that will result in the killer's death. One example of this was twenty-year-old Richard Shoop, who suffered from severe depression and had long abused drugs, particularly MDMA. On November 4, 2013, he entered the Westfield Garden State Plaza Mall in Paramus, New Jersey, with an assault rifle and began firing into the air. People ran from him screaming in terror, but he did not shoot anyone. Instead he appeared to be hoping that police would arrive and kill him, but by the time they got to the mall he had already gone into a part of the structure still under construction and killed himself.

The Wrong Medication

No one knows whether Shoop's suicidal thinking was caused by his heavy abuse of drugs or whether he began using drugs as a way to try to quiet suicidal thinking. In either case, the result was an act of violence that could have resulted in deaths besides his own. Consequently, experts have suggested that in order to prevent mass shootings, more attention must be paid to preventing suicide.

Experts disagree, however, on whether a substance abuser's suicidal thinking, depression, or other mental disorders should be treated separately from their substance abuse or as part of a single course of treatment for both their abuse and their mental illnesses combined. The current approach is typically to begin treating the mental disorder first before starting to address the substance abuse, but recent studies have suggested that a more aggressive two-pronged approach might be better. In either case, experts generally agree that substance abuse can adversely affect the medical treatment of someone with a mental illness. This is largely because patients often miss appointments with their health care providers and fail to take medications.

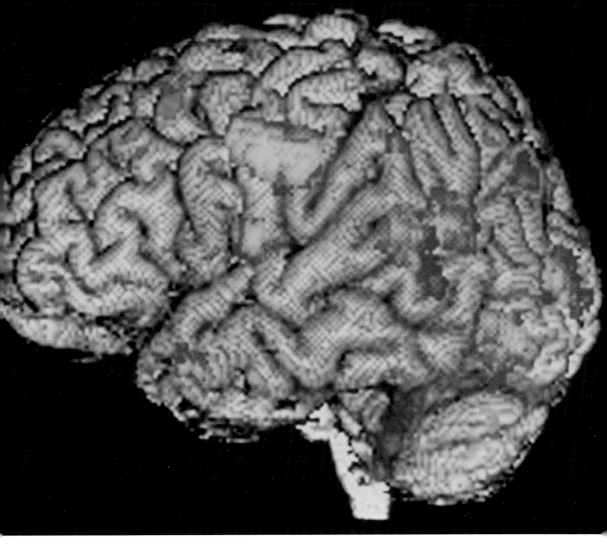

An example of the worst that can happen because someone with a mental illness does not take his medications properly—or takes the wrong medicine—is the case of twenty-nine-year-old Kyle Morgan of Woodstock, Illinois. Since childhood Morgan had suffered from depression so severe that he was often suicidal, and he was eventually diagnosed with bipolar disorder as well because sometimes his depression would turn into mania and aggression. Consequently, he was given medications to balance his moods, and in mid-2008 he was prescribed Vyvanse for his depression because it increases dopamine in the brain.

However, he had a history of taking his medications incor-

The orange spots show areas of brain activity during a hallucinogenic episode experienced by a young man with schizophrenia. Drug use by a person with this condition can heighten hallucinations and increase the risk of violence.

rectly, and for years he had suffered from addictions to heroin and cocaine. On January 18, 2009, he took double the dosage of his Vyvanse, skipped his other medications, and subsequently invited a homeless man, Robin A. Burton Jr., to his apartment to play video games and drink beer. A few hours into their activities, Morgan abruptly attacked Burton with a hammer and a knife, brutally beating and stabbing him until he died.

At Morgan's trial, during which he pleaded guilty of first-degree murder but mentally ill, experts testified that Morgan's doctor had made a serious error in prescribing Vyvanse for his symptoms. The drug increases dopamine in the brain, so it can be used to treat depression, but in addition to depression Morgan was experiencing mania and aggression, and Vyvanse can make these symptoms worse. With the additional dose of the drug, Morgan became so violent that the crime scene was one of the most horrific investigators had ever seen. However, a psychologist also testified that despite his mental illness Morgan knew right from wrong at the time of the attack, and in his closing statement prosecutor Michael Combs placed the responsibility for the murder squarely on Morgan rather than on his medication, saying, "He chose to abuse drugs and not take medications the way he was prescribed."[47] As a result, Morgan was sentenced to thirty years for the murder.

Blaming the Drugs

But others argue that in cases where substance abuse triggers brain changes that result in violence, the substances are always at fault. In fact, when it comes to illegal drugs, Fazel says that if not for drug abuse the rates of violent crime among mentally ill people would drop dramatically. He states, "The relationship between violent crime and serious mental illness can be explained by alcohol and substance abuse. If you take away the substance abuse, the contribution of the illness itself is minimal."[48]

Fazel also reports that according to his evaluation of study data, all substance abusers are at the same risk of committing a violent act regardless of whether they have been diagnosed as mentally ill. Moreover, he argues that mentally ill people who do not abuse drugs or alcohol are no more dangerous than drug addicts and alcoholics who do not have a mental illness. He states, "It's probably more dangerous walking outside a pub on a late night than walking outside a hospital where [mental] patients have been released."[49]

Fazel suggests that genetics might be another factor in the connection between substance abuse and mental illness. He bases this theory on studies indicating that ten times more people with bipolar disorder abuse alcohol and drugs than people with no mental illness do. In explaining the significance he says, "We are looking at two reasons why this figure is higher. One is whether patients attempt to self-medicate with substance abuse. The other is that there is a possibility of genetic predisposition towards substance abuse given that schizophrenia and bipolar disorder both have an element of genetic predisposition."[50]

Media Responses

Experts say that more studies need to be done on the connection between substance abuse and mental illness. But some also say that support for such research will be limited as long as the media keeps assuming that mental illness is the sole reason a mentally ill person commits murder. An example of such a response occurred after Jared Loughner's 2011 mass shooting in Tucson, Arizona. At the time, Loughner had serious substance abuse problems—although there is no evidence he was on drugs at the time of the shooting— yet the media largely focused on his schizophrenia and ignored other aspects of his life.

In commenting on the way this case was reported, clinical psychologist Vaughan Bell complains that the media felt there was "no need to explore personal motives, out-of-control grievances or distorted political anger. The mere mention of *mental illness* is explanation enough. This presumed link between psychiatric disorders and violence has become so entrenched in the public consciousness that the entire weight of the medical evidence is unable to shift it."[51] Similarly, neuroanthropologist Daniel Lende says of the media blaming Loughner's schizophrenia, "This is

"It's probably more dangerous walking outside a pub on a late night than walking outside a hospital where patients have been released."[49]

— Forensic psychiatrist Seena Fazel.

"Popular media reporting portrays mental illness as posing a threat to the safety of others and these continual stigmatizing portrayals may make the violent victimization of an already marginalized section of society more likely."[53]

— Editorial in the *British Medical Journal.*

wrong. It is wrong scientifically, where excellent research shows that the link between mental illness and violence is minimal, and it is wrong socially, where naming a person as mentally ill then closes off a deeper explanation of what happened and why."[52]

Experts also argue that the media's promotion of the idea that mentally ill people are dangerous makes mentally ill people more likely to be targets of violence. As a March 2013 editorial in the *British Medical Journal* (BMJ) states: "Popular media reporting portrays mental illness as posing a threat to the safety of others and these continual stigmatizing portrayals may make the violent victimization of an already marginalized section of society more likely."[53]

In fact, studies have shown that people with mental illnesses are three to five times more likely to be murdered than people without such illnesses. For people with mental illnesses and a substance abuse problem, that number rises to nine times more likely. As a result, it is also far more likely that a mentally ill addict will be the victim of violence rather than its perpetrator. This is yet another reason that experts say a more aggressive approach to substance abuse problems is needed for those who have been diagnosed with a mental illness.

Facts

- Medical experts note that abruptly stopping alcohol intake can lead to withdrawal symptoms—including hallucinations—that may look just like schizophrenic symptoms.

- Studies have shown that alcoholics of both genders frequently suffer depression and anxiety disorders, while men are more likely to exhibit antisocial personality disorder than nonabusers of alcohol.

- According to the National Institute of Mental Health, drug or alcohol abuse is a far more consistent contributing factor to violent crime than mental illness.

- According to the National Institute of Mental Health (NIMH), the risk of drug abuse among people with antisocial personality disorder is 15.5 percent.

- The National Institute of Mental Health reports that the risk of drug abuse among people with depression is 4.1 percent.

- According to NAMI, about 9.2 million adults in the United States have co-occurring mental health and addiction disorders.

CHAPTER FOUR

Should Mental Illness Be a Defense Against Criminality?

O n July 20, 2012, twenty-five-year-old James Eagan Holmes entered a movie theater in Aurora, Colorado, through an emergency exit, where a crowded midnight showing of the Batman film *The Dark Knight Rises* was taking place. Dressed in protective military gear that included a gas mask and a ballistic helmet, he set off tear-gas grenades. Then, using a semiautomatic rifle, a pump-action shotgun, and at least one semiautomatic pistol, he began shooting audience members. He struck or otherwise wounded seventy people in the attack, ten of whom died in the theater and two at the hospital. Then he escaped back through the emergency exit door, and at 12:45 a.m. police found him behind the theater near his car and arrested him without resistance.

Homicidal Statements

During the arrest Holmes said, "I am the Joker,"[54] the name of a villainous character in the Batman movie, and authorities wondered whether he was suffering under the delusion that he really was that character. He also had additional weapons in his car and warned police that his apartment was booby-trapped with explosives. When investigators went there they discovered not only the bombs but paper shooting targets, a Batman mask, a large amount of alcohol, and prescription medicines for anxiety and depression.

During his initial interactions with police, Holmes's emotions seemed flat, and after they put paper bags over his hands to preserve any forensic evidence related to his firing of weapons, he played with the bags as though they were puppets. When left alone in an observation room at the police station, he tried to insert a staple into a light socket. In addition, the pupils of his eyes were dilated enough to suggest he might be under the influence of drugs, and he was perspiring profusely, but the police did not test him for drugs because he did not show any signs of being confused or agitated and cooperated with all of their instructions.

While Holmes was being interrogated, the media speculated about what could have made him commit such a horrible act. Initially most pundits placed the blame on the movie that was playing at the time of the shooting. *The Dark Knight Rises* features excessive violence, as does its predecessor in the Batman movie series, and it shows many innocent people being killed.

Then information came to light about Holmes's mental state. A graduate student in neuroscience at the University of Colorado–Denver, he was in the process of officially withdrawing from the university because he no longer felt able to attend classes. Roughly a month before the Aurora massacre he had spoken with professionals at the university's student mental health services facility about his problems. One of them, psychiatrist Lynne Felton, told campus police that Holmes had made homicidal statements and was a threat to the public, but a university threat assessment team failed to act on this information.

Pleading Insanity

Once the public became aware of Holmes's mental problems, the media began to focus on them as the reason Holmes had gone on a shooting rampage. After he was charged with first-degree murder, reporters speculated over whether he would be considered fit to stand trial. Meanwhile pundits argued over whether mental illness should ever be an excuse for killing someone. These arguments intensified when, during a pretrial hearing in June 2013, Holmes's lawyers entered a plea on his behalf of not guilty by reason of insanity to more than 160 counts of murder and attempted murder.

This was an unusual event; very few people have chosen to plead not guilty by reason of insanity. In fact, in a landmark study in the 1980s, Henry Steadman, head of a New York think tank called Policy Research Associates, found that out of one million felony cases in eight states, fewer than 1 percent of defendants pleaded not guilty by reason of insanity. This low rate is largely because such a plea has little chance of success. In Steadman's study, just one in four of these cases resulted in an acquittal. In regard to mass shootings, over the past thirty years only four of the nineteen mass shooters who survived their attacks pleaded not guilty by reason of insanity, and only one was successful: Michael Hayes in 1988.

Lawyers for James Holmes (left) entered a plea on his behalf of not guilty by reason of insanity to more than 160 counts of murder and attempted murder. Holmes wounded seventy people and killed twelve others in a shooting at a Colorado movie theater in July 2012.

Hayes was tried for a crime he committed at the age of twenty-four, when he stood in the middle of a dark North Carolina street near his parents' business and shot nine passersby because, he said, God told him these people were demons. Four of his victims died. At the trial, defense attorneys showed that Hayes had a long history of mental illness and drug abuse, and after the verdict he was sent to a state mental hospital in Raleigh, North Carolina, where until 1989 he was medicated for schizophrenia. In 2007 he was declared mentally stable, and he was released in 2010. Many North Carolinians were outraged that Hayes did not have to serve time in prison after being released from a psychiatric hospital. Some made unsuccessful attempts to change the law to mandate this by replacing a plea of "not guilty by reason of insanity" with "guilty by reason of insanity."

"I've been involved with cases where six or seven mental health professionals got up and said, 'This man is insane,' and the court would find him sane anyway."[55]

— Psychologist Jerome Brown.

The M'Naghten Rule

Indeed, anger over the idea of a murderer serving no prison time after a stint in a mental institution is a primary reason that juries and courts rarely find defendants not guilty by reason of insanity. Psychologist Jerome Brown has seen this during many years of evaluating the mental health of people on trial. He says that courts typically adhere to the belief that admitting that someone is mentally ill excuses them for the crime, so they insist a defendant is sane in order to ensure he or she will be truly punished. He reports, "I've been involved with cases where six or seven mental health professionals got up and said, 'This man is insane,' and the court would find him sane anyway. Even though . . . he thinks his dead wife that he just killed is still talking to him, and he's asking the deputies when they arrive if they could quiet her down."[55]

However, courts are supposed to apply objective criteria when determining whether a defendant is entitled to plead insanity. Criteria vary from state to state, but most use a test known as the M'Naghten rule, first crafted in England in 1843. This rule states that insanity can be used as a legal defense if "at the time of the committing of the act, the party accused was laboring under such a defect of reason, from a disease of the mind, as not to know the nature and quality of the act he was doing; or, if he did know it, that he did not know he was doing what was wrong."[56] This definition was developed as a result of the case of Daniel M'Naghten, who tried to kill the prime minister of England in 1843. M'Naghten was suffering from the delusion that the prime minister was out to kill him, so he set out to shoot the prime minister in what he thought was self-defense—but mistakenly shot and killed the secretary to the prime minister instead.

In the United States, some states narrow the definition of the M'Naghten rule so that all that matters is whether the person knew that the act was wrong. However, states disagree as to whether "wrong" should be defined as both legally and morally wrong or just one or the other. An example of the latter can be found in a case in California involving a defendant who was ultimately deemed insane. In this case it was established that he knew that murder was legally wrong but he was suffering from a delusion that doctors at a county hospital were injecting patients with deadly viruses for experimental purposes and therefore he believed his actions were morally right.

An Outdated Rule?

Critics note, however, that the M'Naghten rule fails to distinguish between permanent and temporary mental conditions, nor does it take into account whether the defendant poses a danger to society and therefore should be locked away to protect others. Critics also say that the rule is outdated because it was established before experts recognized that there are many types of mental illnesses, most of them complex. Nonetheless, roughly half of states use M'Naghten, while the remaining states rely on guidelines for determining insanity developed in 1972 by the American Law Institute as part of its Model Penal Code. This bases the decision on whether a defendant's mental state substantially eliminated his capacity "either to appreciate the criminality of his conduct or to conform his conduct to the requirements of the law."[57] However, this approach has been criticized for providing such a broad definition that it might be abused by drug addicts and alcoholics who seek to excuse their behavior by saying their addiction made them unable to comprehend what they were doing.

The Trial of John W. Hinckley Jr.

One of the most successful uses of the insanity defense was that of John W. Hinckley Jr., who attempted to assassinate US president Ronald Reagan on March 30, 1981. His defense attorneys never disputed that their client had shot and injured Reagan and three others. However, they argued that his actions were the result of schizophrenia and that this illness had caused him to become so obsessed with the movie *Taxi Driver*, which he saw fifteen times, that its plot controlled his life. In the movie the main character attempts to assassinate a senator who is running for president, and Hinckley decided that in order to attract the attention of the female lead, actress Jodie Foster, he would assassinate a president. Consequently, he stalked President Jimmy Carter, and when the 1980 election replaced Carter with Reagan, Hinckley changed targets.

In addition to showing how Hinckley attempted to reenact the movie's shootout, his attorneys also entered into evidence a CAT scan that showed that the tissue of Hinckley's brain had shrunk, as is common in schizophrenics. As a result, in June 1982 the jury found him not guilty by reason of insanity, and he was sent to a hospital in Washington, DC, where he still resides. Meanwhile, the public became so outraged by the verdict that many states changed their laws to make it harder for this type of defense to succeed, while three states abolished the "not guilty by reason of insanity" defense altogether.

Some people argue that both the code guidelines and the M'Naghten rule are flawed because they address the circumstances of the crime rather than the history of the perpetrator. In many cases this means that a murderer can have mental problems off and on for years but still be found guilty if he or she seemed sane at the time of the crime. This is why it is so difficult for someone to be successful in receiving a not guilty by insanity verdict. It is the moment of the violent act that typically bears the most weight.

However, states differ on who must prove whether the defendant was sane or insane at the time of the crime. Most require the burden of proof to be on the defense, which means that a defendant's attorneys must show that he or she was insane when the crime was committed. But in Colorado, where Holmes was being tried, the burden of proof is on prosecuting attorneys, who must prove that Holmes was sane at the time of the murders. In addition, Colorado uses not only the M'Naghten rule in establishing sanity but a second criterion as well: whether the defendant—irrespective of whether he or she knew it was wrong—could not stop himself or herself from committing the crime. This is known as the irresistible impulse rule, and its critics argue that it allows murderers to excuse their behavior by claiming, "I couldn't help myself."

But there is a way to counter this excuse. Impulsive acts typically do not involve planning, so if prosecutors can show that a violent act was premeditated they can argue that no irresistible impulse was involved. In prosecuting the Holmes case, for example, this would mean zeroing in on the fact that his crime involved a great deal of planning, including buying the weapons, planting bombs in his apartment, and choosing a crowded showing of a specific movie. One of his computers showed that he had done an Internet search using the words "rational insanity"[58] (a phrase first used to explain why a mentally ill person can be capable of driving a car), suggesting that he had a legal strategy in mind even before he committed the crime. This wealth of evidence likely explains why prosecutors decided to seek the death penalty against Holmes.

The Death Penalty

Someone who has been declared insane, however, cannot be executed in the United States. In 1986 the US Supreme Court ruled

that this would constitute cruel and unusual punishment, in violation of the Constitution. The ruling came out of the case of Alvin Ford, who had been convicted of murder in 1974 in Florida and sentenced to death. While he was in prison awaiting execution, Ford began having delusions, possibly because of paranoid schizophrenia, but psychiatrists determined that he was still able to understand the nature of both his crime and of the death penalty. Therefore Florida's governor signed Ford's death warrant in 1984, whereupon Ford's attorneys filed a lawsuit against the secretary of the Florida Department of Corrections—the agency overseeing the state's prison system. This case was ultimately heard by the Supreme Court.

In commenting on the court's decision, associate justice Thurgood Marshall said that the Constitution protects the insane from execution whether "to protect the condemned from fear and pain without comfort of understanding, or to protect the dignity of society itself from the barbarity of exacting mindless vengeance." He also pointed out that although the Supreme Court itself had never before addressed the issue, "For centuries, no jurisdiction has countenanced the execution of the insane."[59]

In fact, the custom of not executing an insane person has existed in America since colonial times, when English common law (that is, law based on both what is customary and what judges have previously ruled rather than on a specific legal statute) was used to guide legal decisions. In writing about the part of this law dealing with the execution of the insane, English jurist Sir Edward Coke said in 1680 that while the execution of a sane person is intended to be an example to teach others to obey the law, the execution of "a mad man . . . should be a miserable spectacle, both against Law, and of extream inhumanity and cruelty, and can be no example to others."[60]

Ignoring History

Nonetheless, as part of its ruling on the Ford case, the court also said that should Ford ever become sane, he could then be executed. The courts in some states have interpreted this to mean that prisoners can be medicated in order to make them mentally fit for execution. In other states a person is deemed sane at the time of execution if he or she demonstrates an understanding of why the execution is going to happen. This occurred in relation to the August 2013 execution of sixty-five-year-old John Ferguson by the state of Florida.

Ferguson first began exhibiting signs of mental illness—specifically, hallucinations—when he was just thirteen years old, and his mental problems worsened after he was shot in the head while resisting arrest at the age of twenty-one. By this time he had

Curing to Kill

In September 2013 the Texas Court of Criminal Appeals ruled that a lower court had been wrong to order psychiatric drugs be given to a mentally ill man on death row in order to make him sane enough to be executed. The defendant was Steven Staley, who in 1989 shot and killed a restaurant manager after taking him hostage during a robbery. Staley's mental state was not an issue in his trial although he had attempted to commit suicide as a teenager and his mother had a long history of serious mental illness. However, after he was imprisoned he was hospitalized several times and ultimately diagnosed with paranoid schizophrenia, an antisocial disorder, and major depression. Prison medical staff also noted that he had delusions and hallucinations. He was forcibly medicated for his illnesses until he became well enough to refuse the medication; however, once he refused it, his mental condition again deteriorated. As a result, in 2006 a judge found him incompetent to be executed and ordered his medication to resume. The judge based his decision on two US Supreme Court decisions of the 1990s that allowed the government to forcibly medicate mentally ill prisoners if it is in their medical best interest, there is no alternative treatment, and they might be a danger to themselves or others. But these decisions were not connected to death penalty cases, and the American Psychiatric Association and the American Medical Association both consider it unethical for doctors to treat a patient simply to ready him or her for execution.

already spent time in prison for committing assault; later he committed six robberies and two assaults but was found not guilty of these crimes by reason of insanity. As a result he spent much of the 1970s in psychiatric institutions, where several doctors diagnosed him with paranoid schizophrenia. Two of them also independently stated that Ferguson was so dangerous and homicidal that he should never be allowed to walk free. Nonetheless, in 1977 he was released into society. That same year he and two accomplices blindfolded and tied up eight people during a home robbery, then shot them all; only two survived. The following year, after having committed at least one other robbery and a rape, Ferguson killed two seventeen-year-olds during a robbery while they were parked at a lover's lane. He confessed to killing the teens when he was arrested for the earlier mass shooting.

Tried separately for each event, Ferguson pleaded insanity only during his trial for the young people's murder. However, both trials resulted in a death sentence. Some people lauded this decision, pointing out that Ferguson's motivation in both crimes was robbery rather than an insane impulse. However, others felt he should be spared the death penalty because of his history of mental illness and because by then he appeared to have the delusion that he was the "Prince of God" and that if someone killed him life would be restored to his body so that he could thwart a Communist plot to destroy America. In upholding Ferguson's death sentence a week before his execution, Florida judge David Glant said that Ford's delusion that his body would be restored was so similar to the Christian belief in resurrection that it could not be considered a sign of insanity.

One of the critics of Ferguson's sentence was Ronald S. Honberg, national director for policy and legal affairs for the National Alliance on Mental Illness. He argued that Florida was going against the spirit of the Supreme Court ruling because, while Ferguson was aware of his upcoming execution and knew what it was and why it was taking place, he did not understand the finality of death and was therefore not mentally equipped for execution. Honberg said that Florida's decision would "chillingly demonstrate the fatal injustices that people with mental illness face in our court system"[61] because Florida's courts had acknowledged that Ferguson was not faking his mental illness but executed him anyway. Nonetheless, the Supreme

"[There is a] fundamental unfairness of capital prosecutions of mentally ill defendants."[63]

— Cassandra Stubbs, an attorney for the American Civil Liberties Union (ACLU) Capital Punishment Project.

Court refused to hear the appeal of Ferguson's lawyers to stay his execution—and right before being put to death by lethal injection, Ferguson calmly stated: "I just want everyone to know that I am the prince of God and will rise again."[62]

Locking Them Up Forever

Opponents of executing people with serious mental illnesses say that it is not enough for these individuals to be sane at the time of their execution. It is also important for them to be sane throughout their legal proceedings. Cassandra Stubbs, an attorney for the American Civil Liberties Union (ACLU) Capital Punishment Project, argues that there is a "fundamental unfairness of capital prosecutions of mentally ill defendants"[63] because often these people cannot help with their own defense.

As an example of this, Stubbs points to the case of Richard Taylor, who murdered a Tennessee prison guard in 1981 after he was denied his antipsychotic medication and was subsequently convicted and sentenced to death. After being granted a new trial in 2003 he insisted on representing himself but presented no defense and cross-examined prosecution witnesses with questions that made no sense. Consequently, the proceedings lasted only two days, and he was again convicted and sentenced to death. In 2008 a Tennessee appeals court commuted his sentence to life in prison. In commenting on this case, Stubbs says, "Unfortunately, it is all too common for severely mentally ill defendants who suffer grandeur delusions to fire their lawyers and represent themselves at trial, believing that they will out perform their lawyers."[64]

An opponent of the death penalty under all circumstances, Stubbs adds, "Although the death penalty is never an acceptable sentence, even proponents concede it should be used only for the worst of the worst."[65] This is also the position of Ohio public defender Tim Young, a member of an Ohio task force established in September 2013 to consider whether a law should be passed in that state whereby anyone who had been diagnosed with a serious mental illness would automatically be excluded from receiving the death penalty. Young says of such legislation, "This is not to suggest that this is a free pass. In many cases, they should be locked up for the rest of their lives. . . . We're not talking about general mental illness but serious mental illness."[66]

However, as evidenced by Richard Taylor's lack of antipsychotic medication in prison, locking people up forever does not guarantee that they will get the appropriate treatment for their illnesses. It also does not allow for the possibility that one day they might be mentally well enough to be reintegrated into society. Moreover, critics of this approach argue that it might invite abuses, since it is reminiscent of earlier times when people who were mentally ill were involuntarily committed to insane asylums and forgotten. Indeed, Taylor was beaten and starved while on death row by prison guards who wanted to punish him for what he had done to one of their own—and given his incapacitated mental state, he was unable to defend himself from the abuse. This incapacity is, to those who argue against holding people who have serious mental illnesses responsible for the crimes, reason enough to treat them differently under the law.

Facts

- According to www.deathpenalty.org, since 1983 over sixty people with mental illness or retardation have been executed in the United States.

- The anti–death-penalty group Deathpenalty.org reports that according to conservative estimates, 5 to 10 percent of death row inmates have serious mental illnesses.

- According to NAMI, approximately 20 percent of state prisoners and 21 percent of local jail prisoners experienced mental health problems not long before their incarceration.

- The Treatment Advocacy Center, a nonprofit organization that works to eliminate barriers to the effective treatment of severe mental illness, reports that according to various studies, 5 to 10 percent of all homicides are committed by individuals with serious mental illnesses, but in almost all of these cases the perpetrator of the violence was not being treated for his or her mental illness.

- NAMI reports that 70 percent of young people in juvenile justice systems in the United States have at least one mental health problem.

- Grant Duwe, author of the book *Mass Murder in the United States: A History*, reports that of 1,186 mass killings committed over several decades, only twenty-one mass killers, including just three mass shooters, successfully raised insanity defenses.

- Like a plea of not guilty by reason of insanity, a plea of diminished capacity calls upon the court to examine the mental competence of the defendant, but it is not an attempt to gain a not guilty verdict; instead, it merely allows the defendant to plead to a lesser crime.

Could Better Mental Health Care Prevent Violent Crime?

On November 19, 2013, twenty-four-year-old Austin "Gus" Deeds of Millboro, Virginia, stabbed his father, a state senator, multiple times during an argument outside their home. Gus then committed suicide by shooting himself in the head. Sources close to the family said that the young man, who had recently withdrawn from college, had been dealing with mental illness for a while. Moreover, the day before the shooting he had been taken to a local hospital after a judge issued an emergency custody order for him to have a mental health evaluation, but he was soon released.

In Virginia such an order allows authorities to hold a person for up to six hours, during which a decision has to be made as to whether the person should be sent to a psychiatric facility for further evaluation and treatment. If the time runs out before a decision can be made, or if no bed can be found for the person at such a facility, then the person must be released. The latter was apparently the case for Deeds. (Some sources say no bed was available for him anywhere; others that the individuals charged with finding a bed for Deeds did not call enough places before time ran out.)

This meant that Deeds was free to go, and because he was a legal adult his father could not force him to go to a psychiatric facility.

Lack of Funds

State officials point out that the inability to find Deeds a bed is unusual. According to a 2013 state study on the issue, which examined all cases of involuntary admission in Virginia during the month of April, the community services workers charged with finding available beds were unable to locate one within the required time in only 4 percent of cases. Nonetheless, the system clearly failed the Deeds family.

Others criticized the fact that Deeds was released simply because there was no bed for him. For example, a few days after the incident psychiatrist Keith Ablow complained, "When patients are deemed in need of psychiatric hospitalization, they are never supposed to be sent home due to a lack of inpatient psychiatry beds. Doing so is malpractice. Such patients can be held in emergency rooms overnight, or even for two nights, waiting for a bed. They can also be admitted to medical units with a 'sitter' at the door to watch them and keep them safe, while waiting for a psychiatry unit to admit them."[67] However, this ignores Deeds's legal right under the circumstances to go free.

Ending Up in Jail

The Deeds case illustrates how difficult it can be for a family to get help for a young adult who is displaying the symptoms of mental illness. And as Mira Signer, executive director of the Virginia chapter of the National Alliance on Mental Illness, notes, "If a family with resources and know-how has difficulty accessing and navigating the mental-health system, it speaks volumes about what happens to people who don't have resources."[68] In many of these situations, a person with a mental illness ends up in jail before a mental illness is diagnosed.

An example is Kyle Zwack, who began displaying signs of a mental illness after he turned twenty-one. He was arrested twice, the first time for assaulting a girl who had rejected his romantic advances and the second time for carrying a weapon in violation of his parole related to the assault. After this second arrest his parents asked the court to order their son involuntarily committed to a mental hospital, but authorities refused, insisting that Zwack was not a serious danger to himself or others.

Nonetheless, he experienced hallucinations and delusions, some of which convinced him that government operatives were after him, and he began to amass weapons. In February 1986 he shot at police who tried to pull over his car and wounded one officer. He was consequently charged with the attempted murder of law enforcement officers and sentenced to sixty-two years in prison, even though he was subsequently diagnosed as being a paranoid schizophrenic and bipolar.

This sentence largely stemmed from the fact that during his trial Zwack apparently hid his symptoms. Psychologist Jerome Brown, who testified for the prosecution that Zwack was sane, later

said that this type of concealment is common. He states: "Strangely enough, many of these people would rather be found guilty of a crime than to be called crazy and so they will actually withhold the very symptoms and evidence that might exonerate them."[69]

Social Stigma

When people who are mentally ill successfully hide their symptoms, they will not get the help they need regardless of how well America's mental health system is working. Consequently, some experts say that more needs to be done to encourage people to be open about their problems. But this will be difficult as long as society stigmatizes mental illness. Many people believe that mental illnesses are caused by some kind of character defect and can be overcome through will power, although this is not the case. Therefore studies have shown that as many as two-thirds of college students would not want anyone else to know if they had a mental health issue.

This is particularly worrisome since some mental illnesses do not appear until a person's college years. At least half of all cases of bipolar disorder typically present before the age of twenty-five. Similarly, the onset of schizophrenia most commonly occurs in the late teens or early twenties for men and the twenties and early thirties for women. Surveys have also shown that roughly 30 percent of college students suffer from depression that they feel makes it hard for them to function.

> "Strangely enough, many of these people would rather be found guilty of a crime than to be called crazy and so they will actually withhold the very symptoms and evidence that might exonerate them."[69]
>
> — Psychologist Jerome Brown.

Focusing on the Young

Statistics such as these have led some experts to suggest that a key part of improving the mental health system in order to reduce violence would be to make screenings for mental illness mandatory for college students, just as certain vaccinations are a requirement for college admission. Others point out that focusing on college students ignores the fact that not every young adult goes to college. The important thing, they say, is to find a way to assess the mental health of as many people in their late teens and early twenties as possible.

Other experts would prefer that early intervention focus on an even younger age group, since studies have suggested that certain mental health issues that appear in childhood can predict a person's likelihood of committing violent acts later on in life. For example, criminal justice experts Denise Paquette Boots and Jennifer Wareham have found that children diagnosed with antisocial or oppositional defiant disorders—the latter of which involve anger, defiance, and hostility well beyond the norm—are more likely to commit acts of violence as young adults.

Assessment Difficulties

Given such studies, forensic psychologist Gina M. Vincent says, "I think people are going toward wanting all their kids to be screened in high school for mental illness and violence risk—and that's a bad idea."[70] She is against this approach largely because it might lead to people being misidentified as potentially violent. Indeed, studies show that the accuracy rate of the screening questionnaires and other risk assessment tools in use today is not good enough to prevent a significant number of people from being falsely labeled and perhaps stigmatized.

One such study, led by Seena Fazel, reviewed data from 1995 to 2011 and found that out of roughly twenty-five thousand mentally ill people evaluated while in psychiatric hospitals, prisons, or detention cells, only 41 percent of those predicted to commit a violent offense actually did so. As for those predicted to be nonviolent, 91 percent turned out to be so. *Washington Post* reporter David Brown notes: "In practical terms, that meant that if authorities used the tools for the purposes of public health, they'd have to detain two people to prevent one from becoming violent."[71]

Clinical forensic psychiatrist Barry Rosenfeld sums up the situation by saying, "We're very good at the macro-level, saying here's 100 people, these are the handful that I think are at the greatest risk. We have a much harder time when it comes to an individual prediction, to say, how about this one person sitting in front of us?"[72] He adds that the main problem is that

"I think people are going toward wanting all their kids to be screened in high school for mental illness and violence risk—and that's a bad idea."[70]

— Forensic psychologist Gina M. Vincent.

Jails as Asylums

Experts have noted that many people with mental illnesses spend their lives in and out of jail. In fact, by some estimates, each year about 2.1 million people with mental illnesses are booked into jails. (This number does not include those booked into state and federal prisons.) Given this situation Tony Zipple of mental health provider Seven Counties Services in Louisville, Kentucky, says: "Jail, in a lot of respects, is the new asylum." Indeed, the Los Angeles County jail system, which is the world's largest jail system, is also essentially America's largest mental institution. Psychiatrist Sara Hough, head of clinical psychiatry in this system, says, "In many ways, we are a hospital." But Steve Lopez, a writer for the *Los Angeles Times* who produced a series of columns about a homeless violinist with mental problems, argues that while jails are capable of providing mental health services, they are not as good as mental hospitals. He says, "Yes, for some people maybe it's better than being on the street. But that doesn't mean that a jail is a therapeutic environment, and that doesn't mean that this is good public policy, and that doesn't mean that anyone should find this acceptable." He also notes that after their release, these people often end up on the streets with no access to regular mental health treatment in their communities, making it more likely that they will only end up back in jail.

Quoted in WDRB News, "Mentally Ill People Go from Streets to Hospital to Jail and Back," WDRB.com, May 8, 2013. www.wdrb.com.

Quoted in NPR Staff, "What Is the Role of Jails in Treating the Mentally Ill?," NPR, September 15, 2013. www.npr.org.

Quoted in NPR Staff, "What Is the Role of Jails in Treating the Mentally Ill?," NPR.

there are too many variables to predict who will become violent, and while some people's illnesses are obvious, those of others can be uncovered only after much digging.

A Team Approach

In fact, it is impossible even in extreme cases of obvious mental illness to know for certain that any particular person will commit a violent act. In the case of Navy Yard shooter Aaron Alexis, for example, many people said after the shooting that someone should have known that he would turn violent, given that others were aware that he was hearing voices. However, as *Washington Post* columnist Petula Dvorak notes, "You can't lock someone up just because the person is hearing voices."[73] Moreover, Dvorak points out that not everyone sees the same side of an individual. To some people the individual seems fine, to others mentally ill.

Compounding this problem is the fact that a person with a mental illness might visit three different hospitals to report three different symptoms on three different days. In such a scenario, an individual physician might see only one-third of a patient's problems, and that third might not seem serious all on its own. Consequently, some Americans support having a central health registry that would keep track of all reports of symptoms related to mental health. However, this would be difficult to implement, and some people believe it would face legal challenges because it singles out people with mental illnesses.

Others support even more far-reaching changes to the mental health system, as proposed by New York mental health attorney Carolyn Wolf and others: embracing a team approach whereby anyone who sees anything disturbing reports it to a threat-assessment agency that would put all the pieces together to form a more complete picture of an individual's behavior. Wolf says, "It's a mechanism like we do with terrorism: 'If you see something, say something.'" She adds that in order to set up this kind of system, "we need resources to do early intervention, supportive services, to triage this information and categorize it."[74]

"We're very good at the macro-level, saying here's 100 people, these are the handful that I think are at the greatest risk. We have a much harder time when it comes to an individual prediction, to say, how about this one person sitting in front of us?"[72]

— Clinical forensic psychiatrist Barry Rosenfeld of Fordham University.

Privacy Laws

Once children legally become adults, privacy laws provide them with protection from anyone, even a parent, having access to their personal records unless they have given that individual written permission. The exception to this is if it is obvious that withholding this information would put the health and/or safety of the individual or others at risk. However, federal law does make it permissible for college or university officials to share personal observations without the student's permission. This means, for example, that professors can tell parents that they have witnessed their adult child behaving oddly in class. Unfortunately many university officials do not know that this is allowed and therefore fail to offer such information until the student is in serious trouble.

But even when there is an awareness of the law, some teachers—whether at the university level or in younger grades—are uncomfortable making a subjective judgment about someone's mental health. For this reason, experts argue that there should be training programs for anyone who might be put into the position of trying to identify a mental health problem. In June 2013 President Barack Obama called for the funding of such training programs for teachers at all grade levels.

Some experts, however, note that making changes to increase the reporting of mental illness cases will mean little in terms of reducing potential violence as long as the person has difficulty obtaining proper treatment and, if insured, getting the insurance company to pay for necessary medications. Many experts say more needs to be done in this area. Studies have shown that if people with mental illnesses have access to the appropriate medications their risk of committing a violent act is reduced. For example, a study reported in May 2013 in *Psychiatric Services* magazine found that people with mental illnesses who received medication and/or therapy were far less likely to get arrested and/or get into legal trouble than those who did not receive medication, therapy, or both. But of course this benefit is based on people not only getting their medication but also taking it as prescribed.

"You can't lock someone up just because the person is hearing voices."[73]

— *Washington Post* columnist Petula Dvorak.

Gun Control

Surveys indicate that many Americans agree that more needs to be done to make it easier for people to gain access to mental health services. However, in the wake of widely publicized mass shootings the public's attention is typically focused on making it more difficult for mentally ill people to gain access to firearms. Federal law already prohibits the sale of firearms to a person who has been adjudicated (found by a court or other legal authority) to have a "mental defect" or has been involuntarily committed to any mental institution—a decision based on whether the individual is a danger to himself or others, lacks the mental capacity to manage his own affairs, or has been declared as part of a criminal case to be insane or mentally unable to stand trial. The names of such people are entered into a national database that also includes the names of people convicted of certain kinds of crimes, and gun dealers are supposed to refer to this database (a process called running a background check) before selling someone a gun.

Critics of this system note that people selling guns privately do not have to run background checks. Moreover, criminals and mentally ill people who have never been subject to a court decision that would prevent them from owning guns are not on the list. This means that under federal law mentally ill people who have entered treatment voluntarily, even in a mental hospital, can still own guns as long as they have no criminal history that would preclude them from possessing firearms.

To remedy this, some states have passed more stringent laws. For example, California temporarily denies guns to people who are in a psychiatric facility voluntarily, to individuals who have recently been subjected to a seventy-two-hour hospitalization for psychiatric evaluation, and to individuals who have recently told a licensed psychotherapist that they plan to physically harm a specific person or persons. New Jersey denies gun permits to individuals who refuse to allow access to their mental health records. Indiana allows police to seize guns from anyone, even those who have never been declared mentally ill, who has threatened physical harm to self or others.

However, states send to the national database only the names of people who meet the federal criteria to be included in that database. This means that someone who cannot buy a gun in a state with stricter laws might be able to buy a gun in a state with laxer regulations. Therefore some people have called for the establishment of a national registry that would contain the names of people who have any kind of mental health issues. Under this approach, treatment for a serious mental illness would bar a person from buying a gun just as surely as if that person had been adjudicated as mentally ill.

Opponents of this approach say it would violate the civil rights of people with mental illnesses and might make some of them less likely to seek necessary treatment. Michael Fitzpatrick of the National Alliance on Mental Illness says:

> Clearly, people who are seen to be dangerous should not have access to weapons. How you do that is the trick here.

A customer provides information for a routine background check before buying a gun. Under federal law, a person may not buy a gun if he or she has been found by a court to have certain problems with mental illness.

Yoga as Treatment?

Given the expense and side effects of psychiatric medications and the difficulties in getting mentally ill patients to take them as directed, researchers have been looking for natural ways to improve mental health. One of the most promising is yoga. Originating in ancient India, yoga involves creating balance in body and mind through certain movements and thought practices, and there is often a spiritual component to it as well. In January 2013 the journal *Frontiers in Psychiatry* reported on a study led by researchers at Duke University in Durham, North Carolina, that analyzed sixteen studies on the effects that practicing yoga has on a variety of mental health problems, including depression and schizophrenia. They found that yoga improved the symptoms of serious disorders like schizophrenia, although not enough to make medications completely unnecessary, and improved mild depression and sleep disorders to such a degree that medication was not necessary. Therefore the researchers call for more extensive studies on the benefits of yoga. Researcher Murali Doraiswamy states: "Many millions of Americans are doing yoga and many millions of Americans have mental illnesses and are popping psychiatric pills daily. Despite all of this, the vast majority of studies looking at the benefits of yoga are all small studies. We did not come across a single study where there was a coordinated effort done by some large agency to really conduct a large national study." This, he says, is what is needed.

Quoted in Alexander Sifferlin, "Yoga and the Mind: Can Yoga Reduce Symptoms of Major Psychiatric Disorders?," *Time*, January 28, 2013. http://healthland.time.com.

You don't want to set up a system where you're barring people who have a mental health history from having a hunting rifle, for example. . . . [And] who's going to identify [which people should be on the list of who can't have guns]? How long do you stay on the list and are you going to act as a barrier from people taking that first step to get treatment because they're afraid they're going to [be] put on some government list?[75]

Mandating Treatment?

Others concerned about the creation of a government list suggest that it might be used to force people to seek treatment or even to send America back to the days when people could easily be committed against their will and forced to take medicine they did not want. Indeed, there have already been calls to mandate treatment for anyone with a mental illness. In January 2013 after the Sandy Hook shooting, the members of the Potomac Institute for Policy Studies' Center for Revolutionary Scientific Thought wrote in a *U.S. News & World Report* editorial, "It is time that the country considers a healthcare regime that provides and mandates treatment of those affected by diseases of the mind. . . . We should view advanced and aggressive treatment of mental disease as important to our security and society as Department of Defense and Homeland Security funding."[76]

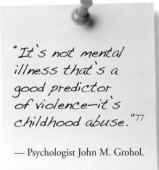

"It's not mental illness that's a good predictor of violence—it's childhood abuse."[77]

— Psychologist John M. Grohol.

But others argue that this suggestion ignores the fact that most violent acts are committed by people without mental illnesses. It also ignores research showing that violence arises from a combination of factors. Psychologist John M. Grohol reports: "It's not mental illness that's a good predictor of violence—it's childhood abuse. Childhood abuse more than doubles your risk of violence alone. And while it shows that mental illness and substance abuse both increase this risk substantially on their own, the real multiplier is when you combine these two. . . . When you put those three factors together [childhood abuse, mental illness, and substance abuse], you have a clinically significant risk for violence."[77]

Therefore Grohol argues that "it would be ludicrous to suggest that if we 'fixed' the broken mental health system, we would cut down on these random acts of violence. Maybe we would, maybe we wouldn't. But it's just plain dumb (and perhaps a tad delusional) to try and sell people on this as a reason to fix the system. . . . Please, yes, let's fix the system. But let's do it because it's the right thing to do—not because we're motivated by irrational fear"[78] spread by psychiatrists and journalists who promote the idea that mentally ill people are likely to be violent. Others counter that it is not irrational to be fearful about mass shootings and other horrific crimes. But they acknowledge that this fear needs to be set aside in order to find rational ways to deal with the complexity of mental health issues as they relate to violence.

Facts

- According to the National Institute of Mental Health (NIMH), approximately 2.4 million Americans have some form of schizophrenia.

- Experts say that suicide is the third leading cause of death among college students.

- Studies have shown that young people diagnosed with depression are five times more likely to attempt suicide than adults diagnosed with depression.

- In its 2014 fiscal budget, the Obama administration allotted $205 million for research efforts and programs to help identify mental health concerns early, including $30 million earmarked for expanding knowledge about gun violence prevention.

- NAMI reports that serious mental illnesses cost the United States $193.2 billion in lost earnings per year.

- According to NAMI, American adults who have serious mental illnesses die on average twenty-five years earlier than those without such illnesses, and most of these deaths are caused by treatable medical conditions.

Source Notes

Introduction: Contributing to Violence?

1. Quoted in *Washington Post*, "Rampage at the Navy Yard: What Happened Inside Building 197?," September 25, 2013. www.washington post.com.
2. Quoted in Death Penalty Information Center, "Mental Illness and the Death Penalty: Description of Mental Illness." www.deathpenalty info.org.
3. Mona Charen, "Mass Shootings and Our Betrayal of the Mentally Ill," *Chicago Sun-Times*, September 19, 2013. www.suntimes.com.
4. Charen, "Mass Shootings and Our Betrayal of the Mentally Ill."
5. Quoted in Michael Allen, "Fox News Says Lock Up Mentally Ill People to Stop Gun Violence," Opposing Views, September 20, 2013. www.opposingviews.com.
6. Editorial Board, "Should 11 Million Mentally Ill Be Locked Up? Our View," *USA Today*, September 26, 2013. www.usatoday.com.
7. Quoted in Jerry Zremski, "Better Care for Mentally Ill Won't Be Enough, Experts Say," *Buffalo News*, December 15, 2012. www.buf falonews.com.
8. Quoted in Mark Roth, "Mysteries of the Mind: Violence by Mentally Ill Is Rare, but More Frequent than in Others," *Pittsburg Post-Gazette*, January 29, 2013. www.post-gazette.com.
9. Margot Sanger-Katz, "Why Improving Mental Health Would Do Little to End Gun Violence," *National Journal*, January 24, 2013. www.nationaljournal.com.

Chapter One: What Are the Origins of Concerns About Mental Illness and Crime?

10. Quoted in Nick Carr, aka Scout, "Memories from an Insane Asylum," Scouting New York, April 15, 2013. www.scoutingny.com.
11. Quoted in Carr, "Memories from an Insane Asylum."
12. Quoted in Vic DiGravio, "The Last Bill JFK Signed—and the Mental Health Work Still Undone," WBUR's Common Health, October 23, 2013. http://commonhealth.wbur.org.
13. E. Fuller Torrey, "Ronald Reagan's Shameful Legacy: Violence, the Homeless, and Mental Illness," *Salon*, September 29, 2013. www.salon.com.

14. Quoted in Associated Press, "Mass Shootings Are Not Growing in Frequency, Experts Say," *NY Daily News*, December 15, 2012. www.nydailynews.com.

15. Quoted in Associated Press, "Mass Shootings Are Not Growing in Frequency, Experts Say."

16. Quoted in *Economist*, "Why the NRA Keeps Talking About Mental Illness, Rather than Guns," Lexington's Notebook, March 13, 2013. www.economist.com.

17. Quoted in *Economist*, "Why the NRA Keeps Talking About Mental Illness, Rather than Guns."

18. Matthew Parker, "The NRA Is Wrong: The Myth of Illegal Guns," Daily Beast, May 26, 2013. www.thedailybeast.com.

19. Quoted in *Economist*, "Why the NRA Keeps Talking About Mental Illness, Rather than Guns."

Chapter Two: How Strong Is the Link Between Mental Illness and Crime?

20. Quoted in Kayleigh McEnany, "Guns Don't Kill People, Deranged Men Do," *Blaze*, April 12, 2013. www.theblaze.com.

21. Quoted in Sarah Hepola, "Loughner a 'Textbook Case' Paranoid Schizophrenic," *Salon*, January 11, 2011. www.salon.com.

22. Quoted in Hepola, "Loughner a 'Textbook Case' Paranoid Schizophrenic."

23. Quoted in Hepola, "Loughner a 'Textbook Case' Paranoid Schizophrenic."

24. Paul Bright, "Jared Loughner Sentenced to Life in Prison; Schizophrenic Diagnosis a Factor," *San Francisco Examiner*, November 8, 2012. www.examiner.com.

25. Paul Steinberg, "Our Failed Approach to Schizophrenia," *New York Times*, December 25, 2012. www.nytimes.com.

26. Quoted in Roth, "Mysteries of the Mind."

27. Quoted in Margarita Tartakovsky, "Media's Damaging Depictions of Mental Illness," PsychCentral, 2009. http://psychcentral.com.

28. Catherine Walker, "Misconceptions, Crime, and Mental Health Disorders," Mental Healthy. www.mentalhealthy.co.uk.

29. Catherine Walker, "Misconceptions, Crime, and Mental Health Disorders."

30. Quoted in Kendra Cherry, "Overview of Personality Disorders," About.com. http://psychology.about.com.

31. J. Reid Meloy, "The Seven Myths of Mass Murder," blog post, September 28, 2012. http://blog.oup.com.

32. Meloy, "The Seven Myths of Mass Murder."

33. Harvard Medical Center, "Mental Illness and Violence," *Harvard Mental Health Letter*, January 2011. www.health.harvard.edu.

34. Meloy, "The Seven Myths of Mass Murder."

35. Treatment Advocacy Center, "Violent Behavior: One of the Consequences of Failing to Treat Individuals with Severe Mental Illness," briefing paper, April 2011. www.treatmentadvocacycenter.org.

36. Nicola Davies, "The Making of a Monster," *Health Psychology Consultancy* (blog), July 30, 2012. http://healthpsychologyconsultancy.wordpress.com.

37. Quoted in Kenya Bello, "Fear of the Mentally Ill Most Often Not Justified," Georgia Department of Human Services, July 7, 2007. http://dhs.georgia.gov.

Chapter Three: What Role Does Substance Abuse Play in Mental Illness and Crime?

38. Quoted in Paul Purpura, "Jefferson Parish Judge Bars Mentally Ill Killer's Release from State Hospital," NOLA.com, May 16, 2012. www.nola.com.

39. Quoted in Purpura, "Jefferson Parish Judge Bars Mentally Ill Killer's Release from State Hospital."

40. Quoted in WLOX, "Experts: Substance Abuse Involved in 70% of Murders," October 14, 2011. www.wlox.com.

41. Harvard Medical Center, "Mental Illness and Violence," *Harvard Mental Health Letter*, January 2011. www.health.harvard.edu.

42. Quoted in WLOX, "Experts: Substance Abuse Involved in 70% of Murders."

43. Quoted in Linda Foster, "How Mental Illness and Addiction Influence Each Other," Everyday Health, April 20, 2009. www.everydayhealth.com.

44. Quoted in Foster, "How Mental Illness and Addiction Influence Each Other."

45. National Alliance on Mental Illness, "Dual Diagnosis: Substance Abuse and Mental Illness." www.nami.org.

46. Mark Ilgen and Felicia Kleinberg, "The Link Between Substance Abuse, Violence, and Suicide," *Psychiatric Times*, January 20, 2011. www.psychiatrictimes.com.

47. Quoted in Amanda Marrazzo, "Mental Illness, Substance Abuse and Prescription Drugs Lead to Gruesome Murder in a Small Town," blog post, October 18, 2013. http://amandamarrazzo.com.

48. Quoted in Randeep Ramesh, "Substance Abuse, Not Mental Illness, Causes Violent Crime," *Guardian* (UK), September 6, 2010. www.theguardian.com.

49. Quoted in Ramesh, "Substance Abuse, Not Mental Illness, Causes Violent Crime."

50. Quoted in Ramesh, "Substance Abuse, Not Mental Illness, Causes Violent Crime."

51. Vaughan Bell, "Crazy Talk," *Slate*, January 9, 2011. www.slate.com.

52. Daniel Lende, "Jared Lee Loughner—Is Mental Illness the Explanation for What He Did?," *Neuroanthropology* (blog), January 9, 2011. http://blogs.plos.org.

53. Quoted in Maia Szalavitz, "Mental Illness Increases Risk of Being Homicide Victim," *Time*, March 7, 2013. http://healthland.time .com.

Chapter Four: Should Mental Illness Be a Defense Against Criminality?

54. Quoted in Thomas Peipert and P. Solomon Banda, "James Holmes, Suspected Aurora, Colorado 'Dark Knight Rises' Shooter: 'I Am the Joker,'" ABC Action News, July 20, 2012. www.abcactionnews.com.

55. Quoted in John Biewen, "Not Sick Enough: The Insanity Defense," American Radioworks, American Public Media, 2013. http://ameri canradioworks.publicradio.org.

56. Quoted in Free Dictionary, "M'Naghten Rule." http://legal-diction ary.thefreedictionary.com.

57. Quoted in Legal Information Institute, "Insanity Defense." www. law.cornell.edu.

58. Quoted in Dan Elliott, "James Holmes Insanity Defense Could Come Down to What Evidence Gets into Theater Shooting Trial," *Huffington Post*, October 17, 2013. www.huffingtonpost.com.

59. Quoted in Curtis J. Sitomer, "High Court Bars Execution of Insane," *Christian Science Monitor*, June 27, 1986. www.csmonitor. com.

60. Quoted in Ronald S. Honberg, "Executing People with Serious Mental Illness Offends Our Constitution and Our Humanity," blog, *Huffington Post*, July 31, 2013. www.huffingtonpost.com.

61. Honberg, "Executing People with Serious Mental Illness Offends Our Constitution and Our Humanity. "

62. Quoted in Tamara Lush, "John Errol Ferguson Executed in Florida Despite Mental Illness Pleas," *Huffington Post*, August 5, 2013. www.huffingtonpost.com.

63. Quoted in ACLU, "Mentally Ill Man Receives Life Sentence After 18 Years on Tennessee Death Row," June 3, 2008. www.aclu.org.

64. Quoted in ACLU, "Mentally Ill Man Receives Life Sentence After 18 Years on Tennessee Death Row."

65. Quoted in ACLU, "Mentally Ill Man Receives Life Sentence After 18 Years on Tennessee Death Row."

66. Quoted in Alan Johnson, "Execution of Mentally Ill Is Issue for Task Force," *Columbus (OH) Dispatch*, September 26, 2013. www.dis patch.com.

Chapter Five: Could Better Mental Health Care Prevent Violent Crime?

67. Keith Ablow, "How Psychiatry Killed Austin 'Gus' Deeds," Fox News, November 22, 2013 www.foxnews.com.

68. Quoted in Laura Vozzella and Ben Pershing, "State Inspector General Investigates Why Deeds's Son Was Released Before Attack," *Washington Post*, November 20, 2013. www.washingtonpost.com.

69. Quoted in Biewen, "Not Sick Enough: The Insanity Defense."

70. Quoted in David Brown, "Predicting Violence Is a Work in Progress," *Washington Post*, January 3, 2013. www.washingtonpost.com.

71. Quoted in Brown, "Predicting Violence Is a Work in Progress."

72. Quoted in PBS, "Challenges Abound in Trying to Prevent Violence Via Mental Health Screening," transcript, September 25, 2013, http://www.pbs.org/newshour/bb/nation-july-dec13-navyyard_09-25.

73. Petula Dvorak, "Let's Connect the Dots on Mental Illness Before the Violence Occurs," *Washington Post*, September 19, 2013. http://articles.washingtonpost.com.

74. Quoted in Dvorak, "Let's Connect the Dots on Mental Illness Before the Violence Occurs."

75. Quoted in NPR, "How Would Better Mental Health Care Reduce Gun Violence?," transcript, January 23, 2013. www.npr.org.

76. Jennifer Buss, Patrick Cheetham, Robert Hummel, Kathryn Schiller-Wurster, and Michael Swetnam, "Better Mental Healthcare Is Key to Preventing Mass Gun Violence," *U.S. News & World Report*, January 9, 2013. www.usnews.com.

77. John M. Grohol, "Myth Busting: Are Violence and Mental Illness Significantly Related?," Psych Central, May 30, 2013. http://psychcentral.com.

78. John M. Grohol, "60 Minutes: Connecting Mental Illness to Violence with Little Data, Facts," Psych Central, September 30, 2013. http://psychcentral.com.

Related Organizations and Websites

American Civil Liberties Union (ACLU)
125 Broad St., 18th Floor
New York, NY 10004
phone: (212) 549-2500
website: www.aclu.org

The ACLU works to preserve and defend the individual rights and liberties guaranteed by the US Constitution and US laws and fights for those who have been denied their rights.

American Psychiatric Association (APA)
1000 Wilson Blvd., Suite 1825
Arlington, VA 22209
phone: (888) 357-7924
e-mail: apa@psych.org
website: www.psychiatry.org

Founded in 1844, the APA is the world's largest psychiatric organization and represents more than thirty-three thousand psychiatric physicians from the United States and around the world. It promotes quality care for people with mental disorders and provides information about mental illnesses through books, newsletters, and journals such as the *American Journal of Psychiatry*.

American Psychological Association (APA)

750 First St. NE
Washington, DC 20002-4242
phone: (800) 374-2721
website: apa.org

The APA supports the work of psychologists, researchers, educators and others involved in advancing knowledge related to the field of psychology. To this end, it promotes research into mental illnesses and disorders and helps disseminate information related to these subjects.

Death Penalty Focus

5 Third St., Suite 725
San Francisco, CA 94103
phone: (415) 243-0143
e-mail: information@deathpenalty.org
website: deathpenalty.org

Founded in 1988, this nonprofit advocacy organization is working to abolish capital punishment in the United States via public education efforts, political organizing, and the sponsorship of research projects related to capital punishment and its alternatives.

Mental Illness Policy Organization

50 E. 129th St., Suite PH7
New York, NY 10035
e-mail: office@mentalillnesspolicy.org
website: mentalillnesspolicy.org

Founded in February 2011, this nonprofit organization provides information on serious mental illnesses, violence, involuntary treatment, hospitalization, and other issues related to mental health and violence. Its website links to a Facebook page that refers visitors to current articles on subjects related to mental illness issues.

National Alliance on Mental Illness (NAMI)

3803 N. Fairfax Dr., Suite 100
Arlington, VA 22203
phone: (703) 524-7600 • Information helpline: (800) 950-6264
website: www.nami.org

The largest grassroots mental health organization in the United States, NAMI works in communities across the country to provide education and support related to mental illness. The organization also supports research into mental health issues and advocates for better access to mental health–related services and treatment.

National Association of Mental Health Planning and Advisory Councils (NAMHPAC)

2000 N. Beauregard St., 6th Floor
Alexandria, VA 22311
phone: (703) 797-2595
website: namhpac.org

A nonprofit organization, NAMHPAC provides support, information, and other resources to state-based mental health planning and advisory councils in the United States. Its website provides links to pdf files of the organization's brochures and booklets on subjects related to mental health.

National Center for Children Exposed to Violence (NCCEV)

Yale University Child Study Center
230 S. Frontage Rd.
PO Box 207900
New Haven, CT 06520-7900
phone: (877) 496-2238
website: www.nccev.org

The NCCEV is a national resource center for people seeking information about how exposure to violence affects children. It also provides a wide range of services to children and families exposed to violence.

National Center on Domestic Violence, Trauma, and Mental Health

phone: (312) 726-7020
website: www.nationalcenterdvtraumamh.org

This organization provides training and support to professionals working in the areas of mental health, substance abuse, policy making, and legal advocacy as they relate to domestic violence, trauma, and mental health. Its website has links to reading materials and fact sheets related to its areas of focus.

National Coalition for Mental Health Recovery

2759 Martin Luther King Jr. Ave. SE, Suite 201
Washington, DC 20032
phone: (877) 246-9058
website: www.ncmhr.org

This organization is a national coalition of organizations that represent people who have recovered from or are recovering from a mental illness or disorder. It also seeks to empower people affected by such problems to have a voice in the development and implementation of policies related to mental health. Its website offers links to websites and information sheets related to mental health.

Substance Abuse and Mental Health Services Administration (SAMHSA)

1 Choke Cherry Rd.
Rockville, MD 20857
phone: (800) 487-4889
website: www.samhsa.gov

An agency within the US Department of Health and Human Services, SAMHSA was established by Congress in 1992 to make information, services, and research on substance abuse and mental disorders more accessible to the public. Therefore, its website provides a wealth of information on subjects related to mental health and substance abuse.

The Treatment Advocacy Center

200 N. Glebe Rd., Suite 730
Arlington, VA 22203
phone: (703) 294-6001
e-mail: info@treatmentadvocacycenter.org
website: www.treatmentadvocacycenter.org

Founded in 1998 by E. Fuller Torrey, an expert on severe mental illnesses, this nonprofit organization works to improve treatment laws and access to treatment in the United States. It also supports the development of innovative treatments for and research into severe psychiatric illnesses, especially schizophrenia and bipolar disorder.

Additional Reading

Victoria Costello and Terrie E. Moffitt, *A Lethal Inheritance: A Mother Uncovers the Science Behind Three Generations of Mental Illness*. Amherst, NY: Prometheus, 2012.

Shannon Fiack, *Mental Illness and Criminal Behavior*. Farmington Hills, MI: Greenhaven, 2009.

Louise Gerdes, *Gun Violence*. Farmington Hills, MI: Greenhaven, 2010.

Gabor Mate, *In the Realm of Hungry Ghosts: Close Encounters with Addiction*. Berkeley, CA: North Atlantic, 2010.

Andrea C. Nakaya, *Thinking Critically: Gun Control and Violence*. San Diego, CA: ReferencePoint, 2013.

Adrian Raine, *The Anatomy of Violence: The Biological Roots of Crime*. New York: Pantheon, 2013.

Lenore Rowntree and Andrew Boden, eds., *Hidden Lives: Coming Out on Mental Illness*. Victoria, BC: Brindle & Glass, 2012.

Eisenman Russell, *Creativity, Mental Illness, and Crime*. Dubuque, IA: Kendall Hunt, 2012.

Robert A. Schug and Henry F. Fradella, *Mental Illness and Crime*. Thousand Oaks, CA: Sage, 2014.

Kurt Snyder, with Raquel E. Gur and Linda Wasmer, *Me, Myself, and Them: A Firsthand Account of One Young Person's Experience with Schizophrenia*. New York: Oxford University Press, 2007.

Thomas S. Szasz, *The Myth of Mental Illness: Foundations of a Theory of Personal Conduct.* New York: HarperPerennial, 2010.

E. Fuller Torrey, *American Psychosis: How the Federal Government Destroyed the Mental Health Treatment System.* New York: Oxford University Press, 2013.

Index

National Institute of Mental Health (NIMH), 39, 53, 80
National Rifle Association (NRA), 24
New York Times (newspaper), 7, 12

Obama, Barack/Obama administration, 75, 80
Olson, Cheryl K., 31
opinion polls. *See* surveys

paranoia, 27
paranoid schizophrenia, 27–30
Parker, Matthew, 24
patient's rights, 14
personality disorders, 34–36
    percentage of convicted murderers diagnosed with, 39
Poddar, Prosenjit, 33
polls. *See* surveys
prisoners
    forcible treatment of, to allow for execution, 62–64
    mentally ill as percentage of, 19
    prevalence of mental illness among, 67
privacy laws, 75
Psychiatric Services (magazine), 75
psychiatrists, availability in wealthy *vs.* poor countries, 25
Psychological Bulletin (journal), 39

Reagan, Ronald, 17–18, 59
Rosenfeld, Barry, 72, 74

Sainsbury Centre for Mental Health, 32
Sandy Hook shooting (2012), 23–24
Sanger-Katz, Margo, 11
schizophrenia, 27–30
    age of onset of, 71
    bipolar disorder coexisting with, 34, 39
    effects of cocaine/heroin on, 45
    prevalence of, 80
        among homeless individuals, 39
    rates of violence and substance abuse in, 42
Shoop, Richard, 48
Signer, Mira, 69
Skinner, Gwen, 38
Staley, Steven, 63
Steadman, Henry, 56
Steinberg, Paul, 29–30
Stubbs, Cassandra, 64, 65
Substance Abuse and Mental Health Services Administration (SAMHSA), 25, 38
substance abuse/substance abuse disorder, 53
    controversy over labeling as psychiatric disorder, 47
    genetic role in link with mental illness, 51
    may mask mental illness, 42–44
    percentage of US murders associated with, 41
    rates of violence among schizophrenics/ bipolar individuals with/without, 42
    as risk factor for violent behavior, 36–37

suicide
    among college students, 80
    by cop, 48
    prevalence of psychiatric condition/ substance abuse associated with, 44, 46
surveys
    of attitudes on mentally ill people, 38
    on blame of mental health system for mass shootings, 9
    on mental illness as cause of gun violence, 23
Swartz, Marvin, 10

Tarasoff ruling, 33
Tarasoff, Tatiana, 33
Taylor, Richard, 65, 66
Torrey, E. Fuller, 19, 27–29
    on risk factors for violent behavior, 37
treatment
    adherence to, substance abuse and, 41, 48–50
    difficulty in accessing, 68–71
    forcible, of prisoners, 62–64
    mandating, 79–80
    percentage of Americans failing to seek, 25, 29
    stigma of mental illness discourages people from seeking, 71
    yoga as, 78
Treatment Advocacy Center, 37, 67

U.S. News & World Report (magazine), 79
University of Texas shooting (1966), 18

Vincent, Gina M., 72
violent behavior
    alcohol abuse and, 53
    among substance abusers, 50–51
    difficulty in predicting, 10–11, 72, 74
    factors in, 36–37
    likelihood of seriously mentally ill to display, 39
    rates among schizophrenics/bipolar individuals with/without substance abuse disorder, 42
Virginia Tech massacre (2007), 21–22
    costs to taxpayers, 25
Volkow, Nora, 47

Walker, Catherine, 32
Wareham, Jennifer, 72
Washington Navy Yard shooting (2013), 6–7
Whitman, Charles, 18
Wolf, Carolyn, 74
World Health Organization (WHO), 25

yoga, 78
Young, Tim, 65–66

Zipple, Tony, 73
Zwack, Kyle, 69–71

Picture Credits

About the Author

Patricia D. Netzley has written over fifty books for children, teens, and adults. She has also worked as an editor, a writing instructor, and a knitting teacher. She is a member of the Society of Children's Book Writers and Illustrators (SCBWI).